FOUNDATIONS FOR CHANGE

The World Employment Programme (WEP) was launched by the International Labour Organisation in 1969, as the ILO's main contribution to the International Development Strategy for the Second United Nations Development Decade.

The means of action adopted by the WEP have included the following:
- short-term high-level advisory missions;
- longer-term national or regional employment teams and
- a wide-ranging research programme.

Through these activities the ILO has been able to help national decision makers to reshape their policies and plans with the aim of eradicating mass poverty and unemployment.

A landmark in the development of the WEP was the World Employment Conference of 1976, which proclaimed inter alia that 'strategies and national development plans should include as a priority objective the promotion of employment and the satisfaction of the basic needs of each country's population'. The Declaration of Principles and Programme of Action adopted by the Conference will remain the cornerstone of WEP technical assistance and research activities during the 1980s.

This publication is the outcome of a WEP project.

G. A. EDMONDS & D. W. J. MILES

FOUNDATIONS FOR CHANGE

*Aspects of the construction industry
in developing countries*

*A study prepared for the International Labour
Office within the framework of the World
Employment Programme with the financial support
of the Swedish Agency for Research Co-operation
with Developing Countries.*

INTERMEDIATE TECHNOLOGY PUBLICATIONS 1984

Copyright © International Labour Organisation 1984

Published by Intermediate Technology Publications Ltd
9 King Street, London WC2E 8HN, UK

ISBN 0 9466 88 00 1

Photoset and printed by Photobooks (Bristol) Ltd

The responsibility for opinions expressed in studies and other contributions rests solely with their authors, and publication does not constitute an endorsement by the International Labour Office of the opinions expressed in them.
References to firm names and commercial products and processes do not imply the endorsement of the International Labour Office, and any failure to mention a particular firm, commercial product or process in connection with the technologies described in this volume is not a sign of disapproval.
The designations employed and the presentation of material do not imply the expression of any opinion whatsoever on the part of the International Labour Office concerning the legal status of any country or territory or of its authorities, or concerning the delimitation of its frontiers.

Contents

PREFACE	vii
CHAPTER 1 **THE ECONOMIC FRAMEWORK**	1
Introduction	1
A Statistical Overview	3
Value added in construction	5
Investment in construction	9
Employment	11
Construction output	12
Imports	13
A word of caution	14
Annex 1 The Basic Relationships	16
Annex 2 Construction Statistics circa 1979	17
CHAPTER 2 **THE INSTITUTIONAL FRAMEWORK**	21
The Evolution of the Contractual Framework	22
The Large Contractor	28
The Small Contractor	29
The Small Contractor and the Contractual System	31
Classification	32
The tendering system	34
Bidding Procedures	37
Contract financing	43
Executing the Job—and Getting Paid!	45
CHAPTER 3 **THE CASE OF GHANA**	49
The Industry and the Economy	49
Administration	53
Pricing Policies and Government Regulations	58
The Construction Scene	63
Consultant organization	64

	Contractor organization	64
	Problems	69
	Procedures and Systems	73
	A Restricting Environment	77
	The Lessons	79
CHAPTER 4	THE CASE OF SRI LANKA	81
	The Environment	81
	The Construction Scene	86
	Procedures and Systems	95
	Registration of contractors	95
	Types of contract	96
	Contract awards	97
	Specifications	98
	Conditions of contract	99
	Problems	102
	Technology	105
	The Lessons	106
CHAPTER 5	RELEASING THE CONSTRAINTS	110
	Towards an Equitable Institutional Framework	113
	The Concept of Contractor Development Agencies	116
	Links with contractors	118
	CDA links with government	120
	Balance, judgement and sensitivity	122
	The Way Forward	124
	Annex The Kenya National Construction Corporation—A CDA in Practice	127
APPENDIX	SOME LESSONS FROM OTHER ILO STUDIES	135

Preface

The problem of 'how to build', like the problem of 'how to manage', is as old as man himself. It follows that the management of the construction industry itself has a long history. In industrialized countries it has evolved gradually, as has the institutional framework which regulates it, to the present stage where it relies on the interaction of a multitude of materials and skills. It is therefore a difficult industry to understand, and many of the institutional constraints that it faces have arisen as a result of well-meaning efforts by non-technical administrators to tackle apparent anomalies without comprehending the underlying system.

Some of the features that characterize construction are the following: the responsibility for design is totally separated from the responsibility for production. The place of work constantly changes and is subject to interference from the weather. The work force has to be mobile and employment is often casual in nature; it also comprises a large number of diverse specialized trades.

The institutional framework makes the industry an easy entry/easy exit one, where firms—particularly small ones—have difficulty in ensuring a steady work load. The industry generally has a poor safety record; the conditions of work are generally arduous, and sometimes dangerous.

Finally, the industry is often used as an economic regulator; because it can be technologically flexible, it can be used to create employment when necessary.

Some construction industry problems are the same everywhere, but others are exacerbated by the economic environment. There is no reason to suppose that the construction industry pattern that pertains in most industrialized countries is necessarily that which is also most suited to the developing country environment. Yet this is the pattern that has been reproduced the world over. This has been the result of historical influences reinforced by inertia, understandable in the light of the other daunting problems that these countries have to overcome in order to implement their construction programmes.

The ILO has undertaken a number of individual country studies in recent years, such as those of the construction industries in Ghana and Sri Lanka upon which two chapters in the present volume are based. However, what has been lacking is an attempt to synthesize and draw general lessons from the experience gained. The authors recognize that Ghana and Sri Lanka may be described as 'special cases' due to their particular economic and geographic situations. They feel, however, that the institutional problems that the two case studies illustrate are in no way unique: they are in fact a reflection of a general malaise. The partial evidence presented in the Appendix supports this view. The authors would like to thank Dr. Ganesan (Sri Lanka) and Dr. Ofori (Ghana) for allowing them to draw on their research papers for use in chapters 3 and 4 respectively.

The objective of the present book is to create an understanding that construction is indeed a different industry, and furthermore that the construction industry in developing countries has different needs and characteristics from those that apply in industrialized countries.

However the authors have attempted to go one step further. Having shown that many of the constraints upon construction industry progress in developing countries can be traced to the imposition of a framework which effectively limits the growth of the indigenous sector, their final chapter—entitled 'Releasing the Constraints'—offers suggestions that should be of interest to a wider audience of policy makers and planners.

CHAPTER 1
The Economic Framework

Introduction

One might imagine that an industry which typically consumes 50–70 per cent of public investment, contributes up to 5–10 per cent of GNP, and provides employment to a comparable proportion of the labour force would be universally well-understood and well-documented. It is unfortunate as well as surprising that, in developing countries in particular, this industry—the construction industry—is poorly documented and apparently almost unfathomable. Given that many of its activities are growth related, e.g. roads, ports, irrigation, land reclamation, this lack of knowledge and understanding can, and does, have serious repercussions.

Whilst most development plans describe the expected (or hoped for) outputs of the industry, few pay much attention to the inputs that would be required to produce these outputs. They will describe in detail the number of hospital beds, the intake of children into schools, and the lengths of road that are expected within the plan period, but this is seldom related to the implied demand that this will place on the construction industry. It is rare indeed for such plans to discuss the motivation of, and constraints affecting, the industry; and rarer still to propose practical measures to enable it to meet the demands placed on it. In general, the end products of the industry are considered in detail, and forecasts are made of the necessary output. Little or no attention is paid to the development of the means to achieve the targets so painstakingly described. The inevitable result is a frequent failure to meet planned targets, which is usually blamed on the conservatism, intransigence or plain incompetence of those involved, rather than a cool analysis of cause and effect.

In the developed countries of the world, the construction industry is generally flexible enough to be capable of meeting the fluctuating demands that are placed upon it (although the cost of the cycle of underused-to-overstrained resources is still considerable). Furthermore, these economies are not dependent upon the industry for growth. A basic infrastructure already exists, and the level of production of houses, schools and hospitals is such that a reasonable quality of life is assured. However, most developing countries do not have as yet sufficient basic infrastructure, such as ports, roads, dams, etc., to sustain an acceptable level of economic development. Furthermore, the number of houses, schools and hospitals is inadequate for social and community needs. Whilst the level of construction output that would be required to initiate and maintain economic growth is extremely high, indigenous financial resources are usually extremely limited. The share of the developing nations, comprising two-thirds of the world's population, in world construction output is of the order of 15 per cent. Further, the construction investment per capita in the developed nations is some 30–35 times greater than in the developing countries.[1]

Besides the direct implications for development, the employment aspects of the industry are far from satisfactory. Thus, whilst the construction industry does offer the possibility of large-scale employment creation, most developing countries rely heavily on the use of equipment. (References to the industry as equipment-intensive do not imply that it is so in any absolute sense. Rather it is more equipment-biased than is justified given the labour-abundant resources endowments of most developing countries.) Very little construction equipment is manufactured in the developing countries and consequently much of the limited investment that goes to construction is spent on imports. In the industrialized countries the reliance on equipment is the natural, *and logical*, result of the high level of wages and the relative shortage of labour. In the developing countries the emphasis is placed on equipment *in spite of* the availability of a large number of workers willing to work for relatively low wages. Whilst standards of efficiency and quality certainly have to be maintained, it is paradoxical, in view of the industry's undoubted potential for employment creation, that on average the proportion of the population employed in construction is five or six times lower in the developing countries than in the developed ones.

The construction industry occupies an important place in any country's economy. It provides an appreciable share of the gross domestic product and generates a high proportion of the gross fixed capital formation. Even in the developed nations (and *a fortiori* in the developing ones) construction is relatively labour-intensive, in the sense that it uses a larger number of workers per unit of output than most other industries, and as such is also important as an employer.

In this chapter the industry is situated statistically in relation to the economy in general. A word of warning is apposite here. Several writers have attempted to go one stage further and suggest that the type of relationships developed in this chapter can be used to predict employment and investment changes in the industry.[2] This can be extremely hazardous if the nature of the causal relationships are misinterpreted, and we shall return to this issue later in this chapter.

A Statistical Overview

In financial terms, the industry converts financial investment into physical assets such as industrial plant, buildings, roads and general infrastructure. This creation of fixed assets to enable other economic activities to take place is an extremely important aspect of the industry. In both developed and developing nations construction usually accounts for over 50 per cent of fixed capital formation. The market for enterprises in, or associated with, the construction industry is, therefore, largely determined by the level of investment. As an example Figure 4 shows the close correlation between gross domestic capital formation and construction output, in this case for the United Kingdom. It is not surprising that the workload of the industry in the public sector is directly affected by the level of government investment. But in the private sector, also, central government action on bank rates, credit facilities and taxation effectively controls the level of demand for the industry's services. The industry is, therefore, intrinsically very susceptible to government policy. What is more, it is used by governments as a regulator for promoting or suppressing economic growth.

The activities of the industry have long been seen by central governments as a convenient short-term means of dealing with unemployment. However, in the developing nations where high unemployment is an established and continuing fact of life, there is now a growing appreciation of the potential role of the industry in helping to alleviate the structural aspects of the problem, rather than as a short-term panacea.

The industry also has significance in the economic balance of trade. It contributes to the level of imports in three ways: by its need for plant to win raw materials and physically execute construction

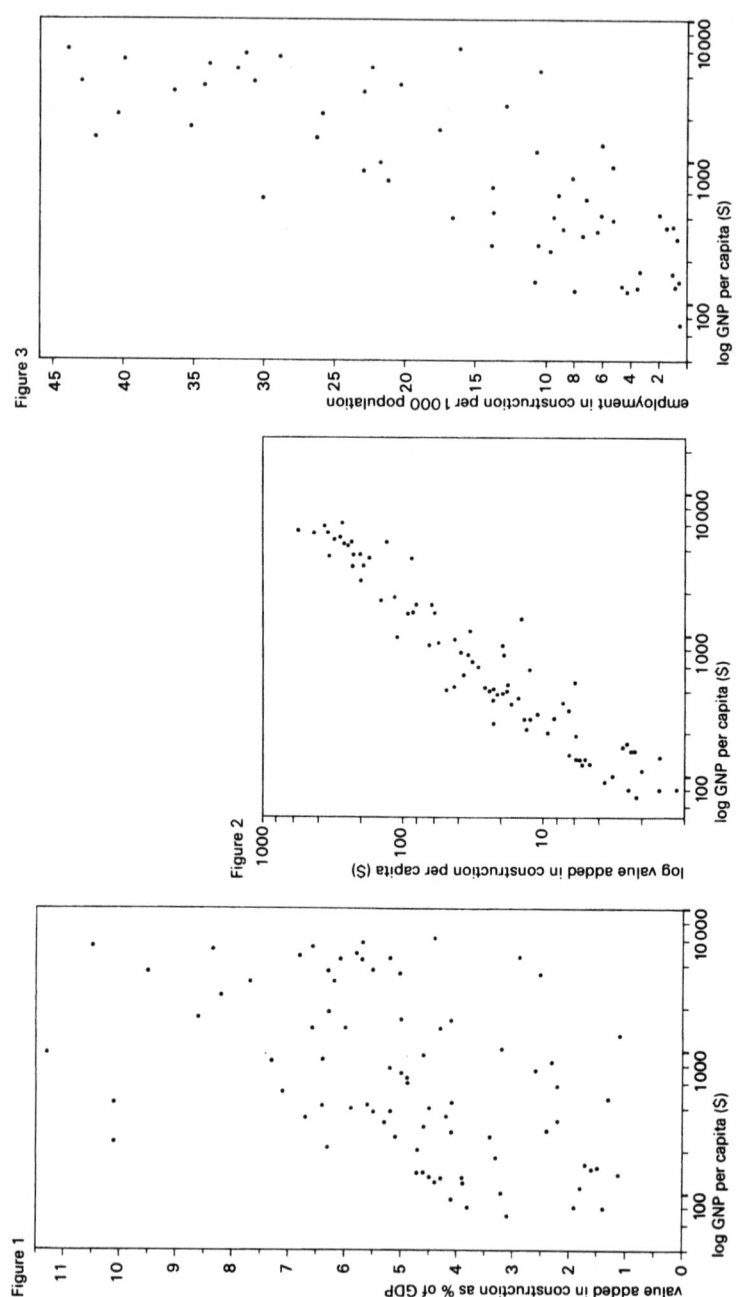

Figures 1, 2, 3 Distribution of countries by value added and employment in construction, around 1974.

projects, by the direct importation of building materials and components to supplement domestic production, and as a result of the use of design and implementation expertise provided by foreign consultants and contractors. On the other hand, it contributes to exports by the sale of building products and the raw materials which constitute the basis of these products, and by the employment abroad of its own consultants and contractors. The overall balance of trade strongly favours industrialized and newly industrializing countries (NICs), while poorer nations are frequently in chronic deficit.

Various attempts have been made to correlate construction industry activity and economic growth.[3] Graphs, prepared by the authors, relating GNP to value added in construction, value added per capita and employment are presented in Figures 1, 2 and 3. In addition, Tables 1 and 2 give a summary of an analysis of world-wide statistics for 1974 (97 countries) and 1979 (116 countries) respectively. The most striking aspect of these statistics is their variability and their range.

Value added in construction
Value added is the difference between the total revenue and the cost of bought-in raw materials, services and components. It thus measures the value that an industry has added to the bought-in materials and components by its processes of production.

The range is large, from as little as 1 per cent to as much as 10 per cent. It has been suggested by Turin,[4] and repeated by others,[5,6] that the percentage value added in construction increases as the GNP/capita increases. It is more accurate to state that the percentage value added in construction is generally higher in the countries with a high GNP/capita than in countries with a low GNP/capita. However, Table 2 shows that the increase is not linear. Countries with GNP/capita of less than $500 have an average value added of nearly 5 per cent, while those with GNP/capita greater than $9,000 have an average of nearly 8 per cent. Regression analysis indicates that there is indeed a positive relationship between GNP/capita and percentage value added. However the increase in GNP/capita explains only some 20 per cent of the variation. Furthermore, if only the countries with a GNP/capita of more than $2,000 are analysed the relationship is much weaker. This suggests that above a certain level of GNP/capita the trend tails off to a fairly steady proportion of between 7 and 8 per cent of GNP.

Table 1 Characteristics of the construction industry, circa 1974.

GNP per capita ($) (1)	No. of countries (2)	VA_c per capita ($) (3)	VA_c as % of GDP (4)	$GFCF_c$ per capita ($) (5)	Investment per workplace ($) (6)
< 300	30	6.1	3.95	16.4	2,930
300–499	17	22.0	5.64	40.6	4,094
500–999	18	45.9	5.32	62.0	
1,000–1,999	9	77.6	5.01	161.0	6,980
> 2,000	23	263.2	6.30	552.0	18,584

VA_c = value added in construction. $GFCF_c$ = gross fixed capital formation in construction.
Sources: United Nations, *Yearbook of Construction Statistics 1966–1975* (New York, 1977); idem, *Compendium of Housing Statistics 1972–74* (New York, 1976); idem, *Statistical Yearbook 1975* (New York, 1976); idem, *Yearbook of National Accounts Statistics 1976* (New York, 1977); and World Bank, *World Bank Atlas* (Washington, 1975).

Table 2 Characteristics of the construction industry, circa 1979.

GNP per capita ($)	Type	Number of countries	VA_c per capita ($)	VA_c as % of GDP	$GFCF_c$ per capita ($)	Investment per workplace ($)	Employment per 1,000 population
<500	A	30	13	4·66	19·5	6,518	3·6
500–999	B	23	44	5·62	99·7	10,974	9·1
1,000–1,999	C	22	87	6·08	187·9	15,437	15·3
2,000–3,999	D	15	239	7·49	490·6	23,571	25·2
4,000–8,999	E	14	466	7·36	861·2	33,787	25·4
>9,000	F	12	919	7·80	1,672·1	57,489	26·9
Total			211	6·14	539·0		16·5

Sources: as for Table 1.

Whilst the value added as a percentage of GDP usually fluctuates within a limited range, the actual value added per capita has a very wide variation. Table 2 also indicates the scale of this variation in that the least developed countries have an average value added/capita of only $13, whilst the developed countries have an average of over $400. The dramatic contrast between African and European countries is exemplified by Lesotho and Denmark, with values of $1/capita and $1,040/capita respectively. Thus, not only do the different levels of GNP per capita lead to an imbalance in construction activity, but in the richest countries the construction industry provides a greater contribution to GNP. For example, the gross value added of 30 of the developing countries, with a total population of 1,120 million in 1974, was some $13,750 million, whilst the construction industry of France, whose total population is 53 million, contributed $12,450 million to the Gross Domestic Product.

The relationship between value added in construction per capita and GNP per capita is extremely strong and, as shown in Figure 2, linear. Regression analysis for 116 countries indicates that GNP per capita explains 90 per cent of the variation in value added per capita. This suggests that construction activity is mainly a reflection of the needs of the population rather than being strictly related to the growth of the economy.

In this context, Drewer[7] notes that various researchers have stressed the clearly defined relationship between construction output and level of economic development. Whilst he does not dispute the validity of this relationship, he criticizes the assumption that construction is therefore an important (and independent) determinant of economic growth, and suggests that this causal relationship may have been wrongly interpreted. Estimates of the rate of change of construction output compared to the rate of change of GDP show no such clearly defined relationship, supporting the proposition that construction output is dependent upon GNP rather than vice versa.

Of course the danger in assuming that construction inspires economic growth is that governments will invest even more heavily in the industry in the hope of achieving such growth. The evidence, however, suggests that a rapid growth in construction output is associated with a disproportionate increase in the importation of construction materials, diverts scarce domestic savings from other productive sectors and imposes additional inflationary pressures on the economy.[7]

Figure 4 Relationship between year-on changes in gross domestic fixed capital formation (investment) and construction activity in the UK.

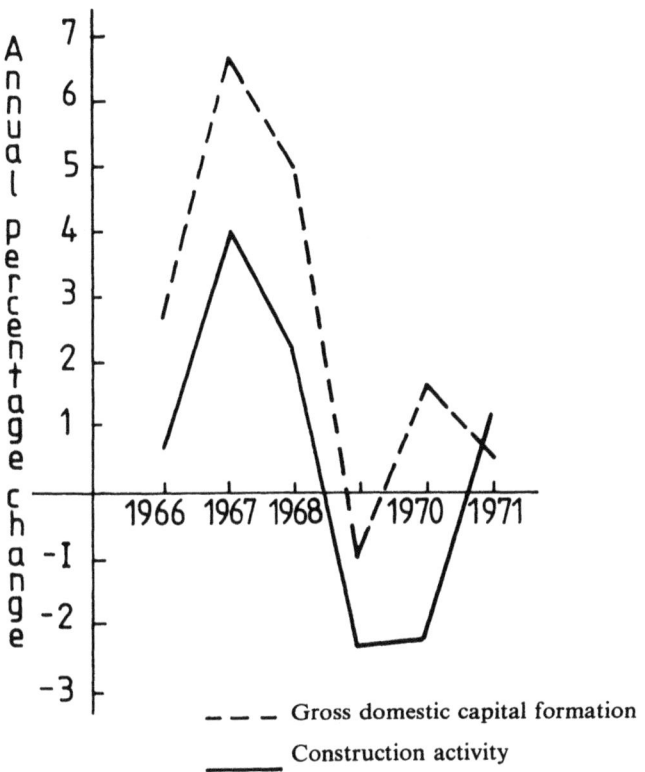

– – – Gross domestic capital formation
―――― Construction activity

Source: UK Department of the Environment, 'Monthly bulletins of Construction Statistics'.

Investment in construction
Gross Fixed Capital Formation is a measure of the additions to the stock of capital in a country. This consists of buildings, plant and machinery and includes depreciation, repairs and maintenance expenditures. Between 50 and 60 per cent of Gross Fixed Capital Formation or Investment goes to the construction sector in most countries, whether developed or developing.[8] The percentage of the GNP in Gross Fixed Capital Formation tends to increase with the increase in GNP/capita. Thus, the percentage investment in construction also rises. However, it should be recognized that in the

developed countries: (a) a larger proportion of investment will be allocated to renewing equipment as industry tends to be more capital-intensive; and (b) there is a higher proportion of repair and maintenance work. The percentage investment in entirely new construction is likely to be higher in developing countries than in the developed. Table 3 shows that in Africa less than 15 per cent of construction output was in repair and maintenance.

Per capita investment, like per capita value added, varies enormously from the developed to the developing countries, as Tables 1 and 2 show. Thus whilst the percentage of investment in construction is at the same level in developed and developing countries, the percentage in developing countries is of a much smaller total magnitude and has to serve a more rapidly growing population. The average investment level per capita in the most developed countries is no less than 85 times that for the least developed (Table 2), whilst the difference in GNP per capita is of the order of 30–40 times. The extremes are Norway with a GFCF in construction per capita of $2,070, and Ethiopia with $6.

The relationship between GNP per capita and investment per capita is extremely strong, 90 per cent of the variation in investment per capita being explained by changes in GNP per capita. This reflects the fairly standard percentage of investment funds that any government, rich or poor, devotes to construction. The regression analysis, however, indicates that up to $4,000 GNP per capita the relationship is very stable. Above that figure investment per capita starts to level off, presumably indicating that there is a point at which the basic major infrastructure is put in place and the need for massive investment becomes gradually less. Tables 1 and 2 also indicate the level of investment per workplace in construction. This reflects not only the natural tendency for developing countries to be more labour-intensive in the construction sector but also—the fairly obvious point—that the level of wages is much lower in the developing countries.

Nevertheless, it is worth noting that the range of investment per workplace is less than the range of GNP per capita (see slope of regression, Annex 1). This reinforces the argument that the industry in developing countries is *over-capitalized* in relation to its economic condition. That is the amount of capital available to the industry in the form of equipment is out of proportion to the level of wages and general economic condition. Unfortunately there persists the idea that rich countries become rich because they use equipment, rather than the truth which is that they use equipment because they are rich. This over-capitalization is more pronounced with the least developed countries. It reflects the general situation that the poorer the country the more inappropriate is the reliance on capital-intensive rather than labour-intensive techniques.

Employment
In all countries construction is a relatively labour-intensive industry. Moreover, it provides jobs particularly for semi-skilled and unskilled workers. The ILO has suggested that, whereas the occupational group comprising craftsmen, production process workers and labourers accounts for only 30–40 per cent of the total labour force, it accounts for 75–80 per cent of the construction labour force.[9] In general, wages in construction in the developing countries are less than those in the manufacturing sector, and this is particularly true of the least developed countries. Workers often perceive work in the industry as a transitional stage in their migration from the rural subsistence to the urban wage-earning economy.

Whilst the amount of labour used on construction sites in developing countries tends to be greater per unit of investment, the actual level of employment per 1,000 population increases as one moves from the poorest to the richest countries. Table 2 shows that employment per 1,000 in countries with a GNP/capita of less than $500 is likely to be about 4. In countries with a GNP/capita of more than $2,000, the figure is in the region of 25 to 30. It is fairly clear also that employment levels off at a certain stage of economic development. Clearly several factors affect this, not least the level of mechanization and the strength of the workers' organization in the industry.

Statistics on employment in the construction sector should be viewed with some caution. Even in the developed countries labour is often employed on a casual basis through 'labour-only sub-contractors'. In the developing countries the proportion of casual labour in the construction workforce is much greater. There is always a pool of unemployed and underemployed ready and willing to take on unskilled work, and it is relatively easy to circumvent minimum wage legislation. A study in Kenya showed that 32 per cent of those employed in construction were hired on a casual basis.[10]

This may help to explain the paradox that whilst the industry is supposedly more labour-intensive in the developing countries, employment per 1,000 population is less. Clearly many factors come into play in relation to employment. Nevertheless regression analysis shows that GNP per capita explains nearly 60 per cent of the variation in employment per 1,000 population (see Annex 1).

Construction output

It is not the purpose of this book to discuss in detail the division of output of the industry. Rather we are concerned with the differences between the industry in the developed and developing countries. In this respect we have already noted that in the developing countries new construction accounts for the major proportion of output. This is quite logical, because in the initial stage of development much greater emphasis is placed on the development of basic infrastructure which will allow the economy to grow. Repair and maintenance have a limited role. This has important repercussions, for it is generally in this latter area that small contractors can gain a foothold in the market.

Given the basic need for shelter, the output of housing is worth noting. Table 3 shows that in Africa less than 1 per cent of publicly financed construction work is in housing. The United Nations Economic Commission for Africa has suggested[11] that, to meet the present and future needs for housing, developing countries should aim at an annual production rate of 10 units per 1,000 population. This figure is somewhat optimistic in that few of the industrialized countries actually attain that level. However, the actual output of countries for which figures are available provides a gloomy picture. Most of the investment in housing comes from the private sector and may not necessarily benefit the mass of the population. Moreover, Table 4 shows that the actual output per annum in developing countries is derisory. Only when countries attain a level of GNP/capita greater than 1,000 does the level of housing output begin to represent a substantial figure. It should of course be recognized that the figures reflect only the formal, generally urban, sector. Dwellings constructed in the rural areas and/or by owner-occupiers and self-help do not usually figure in the statistics. Nevertheless, it is the urban areas which have the highest growth rates of population. Unless the housing output keeps up with the population growth rate there will be no possibility of housing the urban population. As with many other aspects of the construction sector, the solution may

Table 3 Division of construction output in percentage in developing Africa, 1970.

Economic sector	All works	New work			Repair and maintenance		
		Total	Public	Private	Total	Public	Private
Agriculture, mining, quarrying	11	10·2	2·2	8·0	0·8	0·1	0·7
Manufacturing, construction	12	11·4	2·4	9·0	0·6	0·1	0·5
Gas, electricity, water	7	6·6	6·6	—	0·4	0·4	—
Communications	24	16·0	16·0	—	8·0	8·0	—
Commerce	5	9·5	0·5	4·0	0·5	—	0·5
Dwellings	35	31·8	0·3	31·5	3·2	—	3·2
Education	3	2·8	2·1	0·7	0·2	0·2	—
Health, welfare	3	2·8	2·3	0·5	0·2	0·2	—
Total	100	86·1	32·4	53·7	13·9	9·0	4·9

Source: UNECA, Economic Conditions in Africa (1971).

Table 4 Housing construction, circa 1979.

GNP per capita	Dwellings completed per 1,000 population
< 500	0·16
500–999	0·7
1,000–2,000	3·5
> 2,000	6·5

not be more money but reorganization of the use of available resources.

Naturally, housing output is particularly dependent upon government policies. Thus, whilst the regression analysis shows (Annex 1) that housing output variations are explained to a large degree by changes in GNP per capita, half of the variation has to be explained by other factors.

Imports

In most developing countries the construction industry is heavily dependent upon the importation of materials and equipment. This is a serious matter since materials alone account for between 50 and 60 per cent of the cost of construction output. In Africa, for example, as much as 60 per cent of all materials used in the industry are imported.[12] It would be over-optimistic to expect an even higher investment in construction to reduce this reliance. We have already noted that investment in construction is as high as it could reasonably be expected to be. More reasonably one can suggest that there should be a move to reduce the overall investment per workplace and make more use of local materials and resources. Certainly there has been no lack of research into the effective use of indigenous building materials. Examples abound of the possibility of substituting lime for cement, of using reinforced soil for brick and block making and of alternative roofing materials. Unfortunately, few of these alternatives have become commercially viable.

Construction equipment accounts for some 10 per cent of all imported equipment in developing countries, and the amount imported is growing each year.

A word of caution
Whilst the statistics of the industry are useful indicators, their utility should not be over-emphasized. In the first place, it is difficult to collect comprehensive statistics on an industry which is physically dispersed, covers the public and private sectors, relies on the use of casual labour, spans the formal and informal sectors and where the responsibility for producing the end product is separated from its original design. Secondly, any analysis of the limited statistics available should be used to provide indicators of achievement, and not to base policy decisions upon. Above all, the conclusion should not be drawn that all the manifold problems of the industry can be solved merely by pouring more money into it. Moreover, any attempt to support the industry should be directed first at understanding the existing role that local resources play in the industry, and then strengthening that role. If the growth of investment in the industry merely results in foreign-based and foreign-owned contractors expanding their operations, while imports remain at the high present level, then the result will be a continuation of the current state of dependence.

Any discussion of the growth of the industry in developing countries should take as a basic premise the need for the domestic sector to increase both its efficiency and its share of the market. This is dependent upon two factors: first, the structure of demand; and, second, the institutional framework in which the industry grows. As regards the structure of demand, it should be axiomatic that the demand for construction activity be packaged in a way that would favour an improvement of the market share of domestic contractors. An extreme conclusion of this argument would be that activities which local contractors are good at, such as housing and rural road construction, should be given priority over large-scale projects. This, of course, may not be practical. It is, however, often possible to think in terms of disaggregating large-scale projects into elements with which local contractors could deal. The World Bank has taken the initiative in this sense. Large projects have been 'sliced' and 'packaged' to make them available to local contractors. This has, often, resulted in higher over-all cost due to increased overheads and supervision, but this has been accepted as a price worth paying for greater participation of local contractors. The Bank has also agreed to a $7\frac{1}{2}$ per cent cost differential between local and foreign contractors. The question of the structure of demand is one which requires detailed analysis and could be the subject of a separate book. Here we shall be much more concerned with the institutional factors.

Annex 1 The Basic Relationships

An analysis of statistics from over 100 countries provided the following relationships:

(i) *Value added as a percentage of GDP (V.A.P.) compared to GNP per capita (G)*
   For 118 countries:
   $$V.A.P. = 1{\cdot}98 \text{ Log } G - 0{\cdot}009 \quad (R^2 = 0{\cdot}196)$$

(ii) *Value added per capita (V.A.C.) compared to GNP per capita (G)*
   For 116 countries:
   $$\text{Log } V.A.C. = 1{\cdot}13 \text{ Log } G - 1{\cdot}66 \quad (R^2 = 0{\cdot}901)$$
   For 30 least developed countries (< $500 GNP/capita):
   $$\text{Log } V.A.C. = 1{\cdot}34 \text{ Log } G - 2{\cdot}18 \quad (R^2 = 0{\cdot}696)$$
   For 86 countries (excludes 30 least developed):
   $$\text{Log } V.A.C. = 1{\cdot}06 \text{ Log } G - 1{\cdot}41 \quad (R^2 = 0{\cdot}825)$$

(iii) *Investment in construction per capita (I) compared to GNP per capita (G)*
   For 59 countries:
   $$\text{Log } I = 1{\cdot}12 \text{ Log } G - 1{\cdot}17 \quad (R^2 = 0{\cdot}896)$$

(iv) *Investment in construction per workplace (Iw) compared to GNP per capita (G)*
   For 45 countries:
   $$\text{Log } Iw = 0{\cdot}57 \text{ Log } G + 2{\cdot}49 \quad (R^2 = 0{\cdot}637)$$

(v) *Employment in construction per 1,000 population (E) compared to GNP per capita (G)*
   For 74 countries:
   $$E = 14{\cdot}84 \text{ Log } G - 29{\cdot}55 \quad (R^2 = 0{\cdot}574)$$

(vi) *Dwellings completed per 1,000 population (D) compared to GNP per capita (G)*
   $$D = 4{\cdot}32 \text{ Log } G - 8{\cdot}94 \quad (R^2 = 0{\cdot}465)$$

Annex 2 Construction Statistics circa 1979

([1] See Table 2 on page 7 for definitions of Types in column 3.)

Country	GNP per capita ($)	Type[1]	Value added as a %age of GDP	GFCF in construction per capita	GFCF in construction per workplace	Employment per 1,000 pop.	Annual completion of dwellings per 1,000 pop.	Value added in construction per capita
Algeria	980	B	13·0	—	—	10·0	0·4	128
Angola	440	A	—	—	—	—	0·2	—
Argentina	2,390	D	5·2	287	—	—	—	124
Afghanistan	170	A	5·4	—	—	—	—	9
Antigua and Barbados	971	B	6·8	—	—	—	—	66
Australia	8,836	E	6·5	1,060	—	—	8·0	574
Austria	9,107	F	8·2	1,366	68,300	20·0	6·7	746
Bahamas	4,220	E	2·3	152	7,596	20·0	2·2	97
Bangladesh	121	A	5·2	—	—	—	—	6
Barbados	2,659	D	6·6	385	19,650	19·5	3·0	175
Belgium	11,260	F	7·4	—	—	13·6	4·7	833
Belize	757	B	6·3	—	—	—	—	48
Benin	221	A	3·6	—	—	—	—	8
Bolivia	924	B	5·3	—	—	3·4	—	49
Botswana	830	B	4·6	174	10,190	16·7	0·7	38
Brazil	1,809	C	4·8	—	—	7·6	1·2	87
Bulgaria	3,690	D	8·3	—	—	28·3	7·5	—
Burma	133	A	1·1	—	—	—	—	1·5
Burundi	146	A	5·8	—	—	1·0	—	8·5
Canada	9,586	F	5·4	1,390	46,993	29·6	9·5	518
Central African Republic	240	A	6·3	—	—	1·0	—	15
Chad	172	A	2·8	—	—	—	—	5
Chile	1,078	C	2·0	—	—	—	0·4	22
Colombia	1,064	C	4·1	106	15,410	7·0	—	44
Costa Rica	1,843	C	6·4	—	—	21·0	—	118
Cyprus	2,828	D	12·6	650	25,204	26·0	15·0	360
Czechoslovakia	5,290	E	11·0	—	—	37·0	8·2	580
Denmark	12,925	F	8·2	1,810	56,490	32·0	6·0	1,060
Dominica	484	A	5·4	—	—	—	—	26
Dominican Republic	1,041	C	7·1	151	—	—	—	74
Ecuador	1,137	C	7·4	—	—	—	—	84
Egypt	435	A	5·2	—	—	11·0	2·2	23
El Salvador	755	B	4·9	—	—	2·0	1·0	37
Ethiopia	100	A	3·7	6	—	—	—	4
Fiji	1,609	C	6·7	—	—	12·0	1·2	108
Finland	8,701	E	6·5	1,220	38,400	32·0	10·5	566
France	10,720	F	6·6	—	—	22·0	7·5	710
Gabon	3,294	D	7·7	—	—	—	—	250

Country	GNP per capita ($)	Type	Value added as a %age of GDP	GFCF in construction per capita	GFCF in construction per workplace	Employment per 1,000 pop.	Annual completion of dwellings per 1,000 pop.	Value added in construction per capita
Federal Republic of Germany	12,419	F	7·2	1,680	86,000	19·5	5·5	890
Ghana	913	B	3·8	60	—	—	—	35
Greece	4,093	E	8·6	700	—	—	—	350
Grenada	375	A	7·1	—	—	—	—	27
Guadaloupe	1,700	C	9·3	—	—	—	3·0	160
Guatemala	977	B	3·0	176	—	—	0·1	29
Guyana	580	B	7·6	—	—	—	1·6	44
Haiti	180	A	5·1	—	—	3·7	0·1	9
Honduras	608	B	4·6	—	—	8·2	0·4	28
Hong Kong	3,140	D	5·2	425	23,800	18·0	0·2	160
Hungary	3,850	D	12·1	—	—	32·0	8·0	460
Iceland	10,739	F	—	1,980	48,100	41·0	9·0	—
India	205	A	4·5	21	12,290	2·0	0·1	9
Indonesia	331	A	5·8	—	—	—	—	19
Islamic Republic of Iran	2,209	D	3·3	—	—	—	—	73
Iraq	1,226	C	2·3	—	—	—	7·3	28
Ireland	4,412	E	7·4	570	28,500	20·0	8·0	327
Italy	5,686	E	7·4	—	—	25·0	2·4	420
Ivory Coast	1,014	C	8·8	192	30,000	6·5	—	89
Jamaica	1,554	C	5·9	109	7,100	15·3	2·4	92
Japan	8,627	E	9·1	1,810	50,340	36·0	—	785
Jordan	931	B	6·8	220	—	—	1·6	64
Kenya	394	A	5·2	43	10,900	4·0	0·2	20
Republic of Korea	1,613	C	9·4	305	19,330	16·0	6·7	150
Lebanon	909	B	3·4	—	—	—	—	31
Lesotho	110	A	1·0	8	—	—	—	1
Liberia	427	A	6·7	—	—	1·0	—	29
Libyan Arab Jamahiriya	7,262	E	10·9	—	—	11·0	—	790
Luxembourg	7,842	E	10·0	1,410	57,100	25·0	7·0	784
Malaysia	1,620	C	4·3	—	—	—	—	70
Malawi	105	A	3·6	8·5	1,300	6·5	0·1	4
Mauritania	353	A	3·9	—	—	—	—	14
Mauritius	171	C	7·4	235	23,680	10·0	—	87
Mexico	1,749	C	6·7	245	18,140	14·0	—	117
Morocco	657	B	7·9	—	—	—	—	52
Nepal	121	A	6·8	15	—	—	—	8
Netherlands	10,624	F	6·6	1,380	42,215	33·0	6·0	701
New Zealand	6,896	E	4·5	690	34,260	20·0	6·2	310
Nicaragua	889	B	2·9	49	14,700	3·0	—	26

Country	GNP per capita ($)	Type	Value added as a %age of GDP	GFCF in construction per capita	GFCF in construction per workplace	Employment per 1,000 pop.	Annual completion of dwellings per 1,000 pop.	Value added in construction per capita
Nigeria	717	B	9·2	133	—	—	—	66
Norway	11,486	F	7·3	2,070	69,000	30·0	9·0	840
Oman	3,952	D	7·7	—	—	—	—	304
Pakistan	291	A	5·1	25	—	—	—	15
Panama	1,343	C	5·6	201	20,300	10·0	—	75
Papua New Guinea	540	B	5·7	—	—	2·5	0·4	31
Paraguay	1,150	C	5·4	167	9,800	17·0	—	62
Peru	716	B	2·5	50	4,600	11·0	—	18
Philippines	646	B	7·2	84	19,900	4·0	—	46
Poland	3,830	D	11·0	—	—	30·0	8·0	420
Portugal	1,610	C	5·2	185	6,000	31·0	4·0	84
Puerto Rico	4,081	E	2·6	388	27,800	14·0	—	106
Rwanda	206	A	4·8	—	—	1·0	—	10
Saudi Arabia	9,284	F	15·2	2,320	—	—	—	1,410
Senegal	436	A	2·5	—	—	1·0	—	11
Seychelles	940	B	9·4	—	—	33·0	—	88
Sierra Leone	283	A	3·0	—	—	2·5	—	8·5
Singapore	3,829	D	6·2	517	25,630	20·0	12·5	237
Spain	5,300	D	1·6	—	—	25·0	8·0	85
Sri Lanka	240	A	6·6	26	3,500	7·5	0·1	16
Sudan	488	A	4·1	—	—	—	—	20
Suriname	1,999	C	7·3	—	—	—	—	146
Swaziland	680	B	2·2	31	2,200	14·0	0·15	15
Sweden	12,831	F	6·5	1,540	49,900	31·0	6·7	834
Syrian Arab Republic	1,030	C	5·4	206	5,800	36·0	5·8	56
Thailand	590	B	5·3	71	10,400	7·0	—	31
Togo	406	A	7·9	—	—	—	—	32
Tonga	450	A	5·0	—	—	—	—	22·5
Trinidad and Tobago	3,429	D	8·2	—	—	—	—	280
Tunisia	1,163	C	7·2	—	—	—	—	95
Turkey	1,136	C	5·0	153	14,250	11·0	3·0	57
USSR	4,110	E	10·9	—	—	42·0	7·6	448
United Arab Emirates	19,380	F	10·2	—	—	—	2·4	1,976
United Kingdom	7,192	E	5·4	612	26,300	23·0	4·6	390
United Republic of Cameroon	612	B	5·2	—	17,400	4·0	0·2	32
United Republic of Tanzania	254	A	2·8	18	4,600	4·0	—	7

Country	GNP per capita ($)	Type	Value added as a %age of GDP	GFCF in construction per capita	GFCF in construction per workplace	Employment per 1,000 pop.	Annual completion of dwellings per 1,000 pop.	Value added in construction per capita
United States	10,777	F	4·8	1,185	50,400	24·0	8·3	520
Uruguay	2,397	D	4·8	—	—	—	—	115
Venezuela	3,035	D	8·4	680	—	—	—	255
Yugoslavia	2,620	D	11·0	—	—	28·0	6·2	290
Zaire	172	A	3·7	24	—	—	—	6·4
Zambia	586	B	4·1	—	—	11·0	—	—
Zimbabwe	649	B	3·1	49	8,400	6·0	—	20

CHAPTER 2

The Institutional Framework

Having set the industry in its economic framework we need to assess how it is organized to meet the demands made upon it.

As we have seen the industry, as a whole, is an important element of a country's economic well-being. Unfortunately, it is seldom seen as a whole as its boundaries are not easily defined. We believe that many of the problems and paradoxes which afflict the industry, its clients and its users stem from the difficulty in foreseeing the effect of policy and administrative measures upon a sector that does not form a clearly and readily identifiable economic entity. It spreads over both the public and private sectors and is so diversified, both geographically and by the type of activities in which it engages, that it is often difficult to delimit in economic terms. Furthermore, the levels of wages and employment are often difficult to quantify because of seasonal variations and the casual nature of employment.

The industry's fundamental problem, however, can be traced to the systems and procedures related to the distinct division between the responsibility for planning and design and the responsibility for construction. This division is of historic origin and has little to do with ideas of efficiency. It is, perhaps, the only industry in which there is such a division of responsibility. A division, moreover, which is enshrined in legal documents. It results in a situation where the product is defined by the client, the cost specified in a bill of quantities and even the method of producing the final article is circumscribed by various conditions of contract. This means, amongst other things, that the contractor has no incentive to innovate. Studies have demonstrated[1] the inefficiency in the various administrative and legal procedures involved in taking a design from its inception to construction.

Many of these complex procedures have had to be evolved because the products are usually sold before they are completed. Thus, the design often has to be specified in meticulous detail to ensure that the end product matches it. One of the interesting facts to emerge from these studies is that only a third to one-half of the total time is taken up in actual construction of a project. This means that money and resources have to be committed within departmental budgets long before the project is of benefit to the community or the individual. Consequently, the social cost of delays in the pre-contract stage may be high.

The Evolution of the Contractual Framework

The division of responsibility in the industry has arisen for various reasons, both historical and legal. Thus, before we proceed to a detailed discussion of the implications of this split, it will be helpful to gain a clearer view of the features of the original framework itself, and attempt to understand the forces that moulded its gradual development in its home environment. We have chosen to examine the evolution of the British system, since (for good or ill) this has formed the basis of regulatory and organizational frameworks in so many developing countries, including Ghana and Sri Lanka which comprise the case studies in Chapters 3 and 4.

The growth of building and civil engineering in the United Kingdom as an industry in need of regulation can be traced back to the Industrial Revolution with its implications for construction demand resulting from the application of steam power, the growth of factories and the opportunity for transport improvements. The movement of population from the rural areas to the mushrooming towns and cities created an insatiable demand for urban housing and, later, for community facilities. The coming of the railways in the 1830s and 1840s, besides opening new vistas for engineers and contractors alike, encouraged a much freer movement of men and materials and further boosted industrial demand for construction expertise.

Before the nineteenth century, communications were generally poor and the market for both goods and labour was so local that there was little call for building to be organized on industrial lines. Accordingly the execution of building projects was highly decentralized, with each job organized and controlled by a master mason assisted by clerks of works and administrative assistants. The master mason was in effect a salaried building manager, whose task it was to co-ordinate the efforts of a group of craft teams each working to a separate contract (either lump sum or schedule of rates). The craft contractors, each led by a master craftsman, were chosen by competitive estimate. Their contracts normally provided for the supply of materials, since carpenters usually had their own links with timber merchants and bricklayers would also frequently operate their own brick fields. This decentralized system of separate craft contracts operated satisfactorily for several centuries while resources were dispersed, the technology of building was relatively simple and speed of completion was not a great priority.

Things began to change towards the end of the eighteenth century as structures became more complex, and the supervision of the various trades and their organizations began to be placed in the hands of one or other of the master craftsmen who, for his pains, charged a fee, or took profit on the total value of the subcontract works. It was then only a short step to the emergence of general building contractors, who were prepared to contract for the construction of a complete structure, and so obviate the need to make separate contracts with each individual trade. The 'master builder' then employed a team of specialist craftsmen—masons, bricklayers, carpenters, etc.—to carry out the work. The traditional crafts and trades fought a fierce rearguard action, but clients were overwhelmingly attracted by the simplicity of a single contract with a single price, and the new general contractors went from strength to strength.

The transition to 'contracting in gross', in which a single general contractor offers to complete a project at a predetermined price, had important implications for the institutional framework. In the earlier system the master mason controlling the works enjoyed unquestioned power and prestige, and there was little need for formal documentation to regulate the contracts he made on his client's behalf with his master craftsmen.

The new general contractors were less diffident. They could not afford to be otherwise. With much larger sums of money at stake, any single rogue contract could turn into a passport to the bankruptcy courts. A side effect was that contracting became more commercial, and the shrewd man of money began to displace the modest craftsman. These new contractors quickly realized that the quality of the specification would crucially influence the profitability of the project which it governed. A loosely worded and constructed document could turn into a 'licence to print money' for which the ruthless contractor could well afford to bid low, in the confident knowledge of his ability to make up the difference—and more besides—from variations and extras as the project progressed. The growing system of open tendering was a boon for such firms, as few clients would disdain the lowest bid, whereas the old master mason would simply not consider any contractor outside the small circle of craftsmen that he had known and worked with for most of his life.

As contractors became more aggressive in protecting their interests, clients demanded more forethought and pre-planning from their professional advisers. Both architects and engineers started to spell out specifications in much greater detail, partly to clarify the nature and extent of the works at the tender stage and partly to provide a technical document to which their clerks-of-works could refer when supervising the execution of the project.

Contract documents in the United Kingdom thus became more bulky and legalistic, starting with large, simple and repetitive projects where considerable sums of money were at stake. As early as 1805 the Barrack Department employed a form of contract for the construction of army barracks which embraced all the elements of present day procedures.[2] The work was to be carried out for a specified sum according to plans and specifications signed by both parties. Payments were to be made by instalments as the work proceeded, extras paid at a fair valuation and a bond or surety provided by the contractor.

The urge to regulate and control was given further impetus by the establishment of professional bodies such as the Institution of Civil Engineers and the Royal Institute of British Architects, and the steady advancement of the quantity surveyor as a specialist in measurement and the negotiation of prices.

A feature of the British construction industry framework was that it was not imposed from outside, but gradually appeared as a response to the development of the industry. It therefore accommodated the industry rather than constrained it. Its form was in fact tailor-made to suit the needs and priorities of the self-confident British contractors and professionals, who not only dominated their own market but had already gained a significant foothold in many other countries.

The system had not yet developed rigidities, and engineers were sometimes able to implement projects at breathtaking speed. Brunel's achievements as an engineer are well known, but one small episode[3] illustrates the capacity of a relatively primitive building industry to respond to an urgent need, providing it is guided with energy and not impeded by restrictive administrative procedures.

The impetus in this instance came from the national scandal after the condition of British military hospitals in the Crimean War had been revealed, leading to the fall of the government. The Permanent Under Secretary at the War Office, Sir Benjamin Hawes, wrote on 16 February 1855 to his brother-in-law, Isambard Kingdom Brunel, asking the famous civil engineer to design an improved hospital of 1,000 beds which could be built in England and then shipped out for assembly on some predetermined site. Brunel responded rapidly and, on 5 March, wrote to Hawes explaining the idea behind his design for the hospital. Each standard unit was to consist of two wards, each for 24 patients, and it would be completely self-contained with its own nurses' rooms, water closet, outhouses and other details 'so that by no accident can any building arrive at its destination to be erected without having these essentials complete.'

Brunel was a master of detailed planning, still the key to successful building. There were fixed wash basins and invalid baths of his own design, while each unit was to be sent out with its own wooden trunk drainage system. Surgery, dispensary and offices consisted of the same standard units; only the kitchen, laundry and bakehouse were of metal to reduce the risk of fire. By 21 April all the components had been prefabricated and shipped out of England, erection starting on site a month later. On 12 July, less than five months after Brunel had first been approached, the first batch of 300 patients were admitted.

Despite the desperate health problems in many developing countries, it is now almost unthinkable that a 1,000 bed hospital should go from initial enquiry to completion in a mere five months. Why should this be? It is partly a question of money, of course, and partly due to the much more complex medical requirements that any contemporary design has to incorporate. But the growing rigidity of the institutional framework is also likely to have something to do with it, particularly the way in which power and responsibility are dispersed among many different organizations, departments and individuals.

The main split is between design and production, which is unique to the construction industry. In most industries the manufacturer has direct contact with the consumer, and stands or falls by his assessment of the consumer's needs and the price he will be prepared to pay. In the construction industry, traditionally, contact with the client was reserved to the architect or engineer who was commissioned to control the whole process from raising finance, through design to control of construction on the site. The contractor (or group of contractors) had a distinctly subordinate role, much as automotive component suppliers relate to the car manufacturer today. The subsidiary role of the contractor was reinforced by his generally inferior educational attainments and social status.

The insulation of the contractor from his ultimate market had other ramifications. While firms operating in other product areas of a market economy face the problem of selling to a wholesale or retail market, they have the satisfaction of knowing that, once a market share has been established, demand can be forecast with reasonable accuracy and resources can be mobilized to meet it. However the contractor has to tender for work in the knowledge that only 1 in 10 or 1 in 20 of his bids are likely to be successful. Thus he is forced to tender for 10 or 20 times as much as he feels able to cope with, with the risk that at any given time he could be faced with a workload far greater or far less than the capacity of his organization. To these dangers must be added the endemic 'feast and famine' nature of construction demand, much of which emanates from the public sector capital budget, where spending can fluctuate wildly according to national economic conditions.

Fortunately for them, British contractors faced no competition in their home market, and were wily enough to accommodate themselves to the distinctly inferior position accorded to them in the specifications and contract documents that governed their commercial activities. How did they do it? As early exponents of lateral thinking, they recognized that an apparent weakness could become a strength. Clients and their professional advisers had eagerly piled most of the risks in the construction process onto the backs of the contractors, and by opting for 'contracting in gross' had concentrated them. As anyone who has ever paid an insurance premium knows, risk transference has to be paid for and, in the long run, well-managed insurance companies can grow rich by spreading and reducing the risks that they cover. Thus, while weak contractors went to the wall, others were quietly building their financial, managerial and technical skills to assess and cope with the risks they were in business to surmount.

In Britain, at least, the outcome was a reasonably stable construction environment, in which the apparently overwhelming contractual power of the architect or engineer was offset by the formidable practical financial and constructional skills of the contractor. The weakness was that the system precluded the client from benefitting from the contractor's skills at the all-important design stage, leading eventually to the growth of management contracting (ironically, resurrecting on a larger scale the original system of a salaried master mason which applied in the Middle Ages).

Most contractors, meanwhile, contented themselves with attempting to complete their jobs in the shortest possible time, with the least possible outlay of resources. This was no easy task, for the market remained competitive, and clients generally obtained a better and cheaper service by employing contractors than by recruiting their own direct labour forces. Whilst British contractors have become acclimatized to the inferior status accorded them in contract documents, indigenous developing country contractors have not been able to evolve with and within their regulatory framework in the same way. Indeed their inexperience has caused the designer and/or client to feel that it is therefore necessary to lay down fairly strict regulations regarding the way in which the 'contractor' is hired to carry out and complete the work. Whilst, particularly in recent years, there has been strong pressure from contractors' organizations to limit the contractors' responsibility, these have met with limited success. Certain concessions have been given by aid agencies and governments; however these have been given grudgingly. This is basically because contractors have always been viewed as inherently dishonest, only concerned with making the most money for the least amount of work. In manufacturing, in general, the manufacturer's profit depends upon the quality of the product he produces and the number he can sell. In the case of a contractor, however, the only way he makes a profit is by managing to complete the job in the shortest possible time with the least outlay of resources. This has automatically led to a situation where contractors are well-versed in the minutiae of contract documents and of shifting their money around within the contract to ensure that their cash-flow works to their advantage.

Historically, the industry has been provided with an institutional framework which is not necessarily optimum. In addition, it has problems related to the dispersal of production, the casual nature of its labour force and consequent difficulties in framing adequate legislation covering industrial relations and conditions of work.

The industry in developing countries shares many of the problems of its counterpart in the developed countries. However, these tend to be exacerbated by an impoverished and unpredictable economic environment. The structure in developing countries is an extreme version of its developed-country counterpart. There is a small number of large companies—often foreign-owned—who carry out the majority of the work. There is also a large number of small contractors. In marked contrast to the developed countries, however, there are few medium-size enterprises. The small contractors, therefore, are generally cut off both financially and technically from the larger firms, and there is very little possibility for them to grow. Furthermore, there are far fewer contractors in the industry in the developing countries than in the developed, whether measured per number of population or by value of output. For example, the number of construction enterprises per million population is 17 for 23 countries with a per capita GNP less than $500, as against an average of 777 per million population for 14 of the most industrialized countries: a ratio of 46:1. The equivalent ratio of value added per capita is 22:1. A study in Kenya showed that of the 1,500 registered construction establishments only 154 had more than 50 employees, accounting for over 80 per cent of the construction output.[4]

The Large Contractor

At the large end of the spectrum, there are contractors of three types:

(i) International contractors, usually working on large projects.
(ii) Joint venture contractors working on similar projects, some of which may be locally financed.
(iii) Local contractors (including state corporations) working on large national government and private contracts.

All three categories will have similar financial and organizational structures, which is hardly surprising since, as indicated above, they are all descended from the same stock, and they are all working within the same kind of contractual framework.

An important feature of the operation of the large local contractor is the extent to which the work is executed through subcontractors, and this has widespread implications which will be examined later. These subcontractors are essentially suppliers of skilled labour only, and generally do not supply materials or equipment, which remain the responsibility of the main contractor. This is not to imply that they are only agents for the supply of labour—they are more than that, since they undertake to carry out certain sections of the work for a fixed price or at an agreed rate. Thus the carpentry subcontractor will agree to fix the centering for a bridge span at a certain price, with the main contractor supplying the necessary timber, scaffolding etc., but with the subcontractor supplying and paying all the labour, for which the main contractor accepts no responsibility. An important consequence of this is that this labour does not appear on the payroll of the main contractor.

This type of subcontractor constitutes an informal group within the formal organization of the main contractor, and will be bound together by traditional ties of craftsmanship, tribe, caste, religion and so on. Operating as it does in a competitive market, and often with a high demand for its skills, this group has a vested interest in restricting membership, and is thus not very susceptible to change.

The implication of the foregoing is that the large contractor operates in the tradition of his counterpart in the industrialized world, where the emphasis is on labour-saving; the system of 'labour-only subcontracting' removes from him most of the problems associated with the management of men rather than machines; the subcontractors themselves have a vested interest in maintaining their exclusiveness.

The Small Contractor

In the almost complete absence of statistics, and having regard to the great diversity of countries, it is impossible to define quantitatively what is meant by a small contractor. It is generally understood to mean one who is capable of small-scale works only, such as simple buildings, rural road construction and improvement, small span bridges, culverts and so forth. He may be a carpenter or mason possessed of the initiative to set up business on his own, although this is more likely to be the case in building than in road construction.

Alternatively, he may be an entrepreneur to whom contracting is merely one outlet for the capacity for seizing opportunities, taking risks, adapting and working hard which characterize his kind. Whether he be one or the other, entry into or exit from the industry is remarkably easy. In the words of the ILO study of labour-intensive road construction in the Islamic Republic of Iran[5] '. . . it is possible to build a road with no more than a telephone, so to speak, while holding one or more other jobs as well . . .'. This type of contractor has no real commitment to the industry, and is not therefore particularly interested in the investment in human resources which is necessary if long-term improvements are to be achieved, particularly in view of the greater difficulty of managing people compared to managing machines. Furthermore, banks generally regard equipment as a better risk than people, so a contractor with limited capital resources will find it is easier to obtain credit for the purchase or hire of plant than for the payment of wages.

Apart from the wide diversity in size of its constituent members, the industry also suffers from functional divisions. First and foremost, the split of responsibility for design and production is a natural constraint to efficiency and innovation. Unlike a producer of goods in any other industry, the contractor has virtually no say in the design of the product he is to produce. He is, however, totally responsible for its performance and quality. Furthermore, the system of competitive bidding does little or nothing to alleviate the constraints. In theory, the system of accepting the least cost bid should produce efficiency. However, contractors—and particularly small ones—have very little room for manoeuvre in pricing a tender. The design is fixed, materials prices quoted by merchants are much the same (although longer-established and financially well-endowed contractors can secure useful discounts and credit facilities), while the costs of equipment (whether owned or hired) are likely to be much the same from one firm to another. A contractor, therefore, makes his profit on five factors:

(i) Limiting his overhead costs.
(ii) Increasing labour productivity.
(iii) More effective site organisation.
(iv) Shrewd purchasing.
(v) Risk anticipation.

In relation to a small contractor in developing countries, this does not provide much scope. His overheads are probably already pared down to the minimum, he will generally draw on the same pool of labour as all other small contractors; that leaves the possibilities of more effectively managing his site operations and using his financial acumen. Thus, the least price tender system may merely award the contract to the contractor with the poorest appreciation of the costs and risks of carrying out the work. Furthermore, the system ensures that the traditional methods are used and innovation is suppressed, as anything but the conventional methods imply a risk of increasing costs and thereby losing the tender.

Therefore, because of its internal structure and procedures the industry in developing countries is, as Johri and Pandey say, 'capable of quantitative expansion but not of qualitative change'.[6] Unfortunately, government attitude to the industry generally reinforces this conservatism. The industry is often used as an economic regulator for it is easier to slow down and accelerate programmes in construction than in, say, the manufacturing sectors. Consequently, contractors rarely have continuity of work, which not only means that in general they are not prepared to deviate from their traditional methods, but also that they continue to rely on casual labour which can be laid off or taken on at will. This has the effect that there is little long-term employment in the sector, which reinforces the emphasis on the use of equipment and discourages the emergence of a reliable construction labour force.

The Small Contractor and the Contractual System

In the developed countries contractual procedures have been developed, modified and improved in relation to the emerging needs of the industry itself and the change in social and economic circumstances. Whilst contractors are not necessarily lauded as a group of social reformers, they are at least recognised as important instruments of economic development. Moreover, they are powerful enough to ensure that their contractual relations with clients are regulated on an equitable basis. Such financial safeguards demanded by clients and embodied in the conditions of contract may be biased, but contractors have sufficient financial and managerial capacity to protect themselves from exploitation.

In the developing countries, contractors do not have the same status in society. A contractor is often viewed as 'an unpatriotic, dishonest businessman who, given half a chance, would either use shoddy materials, leave out some parts of structure, make unjustified claims or abscond with advances or loans paid to him or influence consultants to certify unjustified payments to him'.[7] Thus their contractual obligations are consequently more severe so as to ensure that money entrusted to them is not wasted. Unfortunately, these obligations do not discriminate between the *bona fide* contractor eager to obtain work and effectively execute it, and those with more dubious objectives. Moreover, they generally do not have the financial and managerial ability to cope with them. We discuss the implications of this approach in greater detail in Chapter 5.

Classification
Partly due to its risky nature, contracting is an easy entry/easy exit industry, with a constant supply of hopeful newcomers attracted by the apparently high profits enjoyed by established firms and ignoring the less-encouraging examples who have fallen by the wayside. This plentiful supply of would-be contractors might seem a boon for clients seeking more competitive bids. The more thoughtful among them, however, have learned that open tendering with automatic acceptance of the lowest bidder is a recipe for chaos. If the lowest bidder is incompetent (or just too short of cash to buy materials or pay labour wages) the client is the inevitable long-term loser. Supervision has to be much tighter (thus more costly), delays and poor co-operation are likely and, should the contractor finally fail, the imposition of financial penalties is scant compensation for being left with an unfinished project that is urgently needed. Government (the main client) can regulate entry to the industry most effectively by registering all contractors, and classifying them according to the value (and sometimes the type) of work for which they may tender. The criteria for classification are generally previous work record, financial status, plant inventory and managerial/technical skills. The weighting accorded to these criteria varies from country to country, sometimes irrationally. For example, the requirement that contractors should own a large stock of plant and equipment is borrowed from standard practice in industrialized countries, and can run counter to a policy of encouraging employment creation through labour-based technologies.

Without suggesting that all construction activities can be executed economically using labour-based methods, it is certainly true to say that these methods are viable for a much wider range of activities than in the developed world. In certain countries, like India, these methods are the rule for even the largest types of project. The level of plant-holding criteria therefore must be related to the economic circumstances of a developing country where reliance on equipment is economically untenable. A criticism of the plant-holding criteria, unrelated to technological choice, is that they encourage an over-capitalisation of small contractors. As there are generally too many small contractors chasing too few jobs, the result of an insistence on certain pieces of equipment is an under-utilisation of such equipment and, by implication, a surplus of imported machinery.

Classification systems are expensive to set up and maintain, since inspection is needed to ensure that the data supplied by contractors is genuine, and the classification must be regularly updated as new contractors apply and as already registered contractors fall away or become incapable of carrying out work. It must also be revised in relation to the increased cost of projects. A contractor registered 5 years ago as being able to carry out work up to $300,000 will now be able to carry out work up to $500,000, not because he has improved his capability but purely because of inflation.

If such a system is allowed to degenerate into pointless bureaucracy, it may well do more harm than good. For instance, in *Bangladesh*[8] it is reported that the criteria for registration are somewhat vague and the register has little practical significance since, once accepted, the contractor remains on the list merely by paying an annual fee. It is of interest that the classification criteria in Bangladesh relate only to financial and technical capability and number of staff employed. Equipment is not an issue here, as most contractors do not own plant but hire it from the government department for whom they are working.

In the *Syrian Arab Republic* there is a classification system but it is so outdated that few contractors fail to achieve the highest grading.

In the *Republic of Korea*,[9] where registration is on the basis of an annual renewable licence, the financial requirements (in terms of paid-up capital) for established firms is half that for newcomers. Firms are classified according to the value of work carried out in the previous two years, or ten times the paid-up capital or assets, whichever is smaller.

Prior to the revolution in the *Islamic Republic of Iran*[9] the major problem was that far too many contractors were registered. This led to a situation where it was extremely difficult for new contractors to become registered. Consequently, illegal expedients such as 'buying' contracts from established contractors no longer capable of doing the work were resorted to. A new system was introduced to try and improve the situation. This graded construction firms on a points system. Points were awarded for: (a) technical personnel, organization and management; (b) previous performance record; and (c) financial and credit status. No consideration was given to the ownership of equipment, partly because it was assumed to be covered by the three factors and partly because it had proved virtually impossible to verify claims to ownership.

In *Ethiopia*[9] the development of the domestic sector is of fairly recent origin, most of the work—particularly prior to the revolution—being carried out by foreign or foreign-owned contractors. In the early 1970s, however, a registration system was introduced which was based on the level of fixed assets, the number of professional staff and ownership of equipment, the latter requirement being that sufficient equipment is owned 'to adequately perform works at the level at which he is applying'.

A points system is also used in the *Philippines*,[10] virtually equal weight being given to experience, quality of personnel and financial capability. The lower the number of points, the lower the classification. This, unfortunately, has the effect that the lowest classification incorporates contractors who may be incapable of carrying out good work.

Whilst the points system has the failing of being subjective, at least it provides a rational basis for selection where none existed before. A points system related to technical expertise, credit facility and financial assets could be used as a minimum entry criteria. This could then be augmented by points for experience as, and when, the contractor received work.

The classification system does not provide a 'select' list of contractors. What it does do is to provide a group of contractors who, in theory, at least, should be capable of executing work. This allows the client to select from within that list those who are to be invited to tender.

The tendering system

The object of the tendering system is, in theory at least, to select from a group of tenderers the one who can carry out the work for the least cost. This simple system has various derivatives.

It is generally accepted that to put out an open tender is counter-productive. It gives the appearance that, by heightened competition, the least cost will result. In fact, because of the lack of experience of many small contractors, it often results in a lowest tender which is either totally unrealistic or impractical. Contractors interviewed in

Thailand pointed out[11] that the system of least-cost tendering often drives away technically competent contractors. They recognize that, particularly in times of economic recession, many contractors will put in unrealistically low tenders in order to ensure that they obtain the job. The selected tender system at least allows the client a measure of choice. Indeed one key advantage of an effective classification system is that it can encourage the development of a reasonable spread of contractors by permitting firms to tender only in their own category, and perhaps in one or two lower ones. However, when restrictions are not applied and work is short, large firms can drive their smaller brethren out of business by 'downward plundering' of work in lower categories. This has been a feature in Bangladesh,[8] Nepal[12] and, most blatantly, in the United Republic of Cameroon[13] where, despite an eight-tier classification 'between 1972 and 1977, over 70 per cent of all building contracts were let to contractors from Group A and in the two years 1974–5 and 1975–6 nearly 80 per cent of all contracts let in Groups B to H were won by contractors from Group A'.

Downward plundering is encouraged by short-sighted clients in most countries who, when demand is depressed, deliberately exploit the situation by circulating the few available contracts to an ever-wider range of potential bidders. In the short run the client gains by stimulating highly competitive bids which scarcely cover overheads, let alone offer the possibility of profit to the 'successful' bidder. In the end the exploiters pay the price, with a gradual weakening of the local construction sector which will only become apparent when demand suddenly jerks upwards. Then it will be the exploiters' turn to be exploited, as the few surviving contractors ruthlessly recoup their earlier losses and urgently needed projects are delayed as the industry simply lacks the capacity to respond rapidly after a period of retrenchment.

In theory, at least, a good classification system will at least ensure that a reasonable catchment of competent contractors is available for jobs of various sizes and degrees of technical complexity. Even so every class, except perhaps the highest, will contain a large number of firms, only a few of which are likely to be fully suitable for any particular project at any particular time. Thus there are advantages for the client in moving further from fully-open tendering to choosing a selected list of invited bidders for each project, forming a group of firms that have both the specific experience and the current spare capacity to undertake the works competently. This saves the embarrassment of turning down ludicrously low bids from inexperienced firms, and encourages the invited firms to take more care in preparing well-calculated estimates than they would in an open tender lottery with perhaps hundreds of other bidders. Selected tender systems also offer the opportunity to provide reasonable continuity of work to firms giving satisfactory service, thereby enabling them to invest in equipment, training and improved systems in the reasonable expectation that the resulting overheads will be recovered. In the *Republic of Korea*[14] a contractor effectively executing a project is often given the option to negotiate for a second contract, providing his unit prices are within certain limits.

Whilst selected tendering solves some of the problems of open tendering, it may still be too sophisticated for an infant construction industry. A World Bank team have argued[15] that in the initial stage of development a group of contractors should be chosen by a contractor-support organization and work would be reserved for them. Contracts would be worked out with individual contractors on a cost-plus basis. Only when contractors had been weaned into the system would selected tendering be introduced. This approach has its attractions. However, if the system is so bad that one has to circumvent it in this manner, would it not be better to change it? A more rational view is that a certain measure of 'hand-holding' should take place, but that a measure of competition is useful even at the very early stage. We pursue this question further in Chapter 5.

At this stage it is worth making a few points regarding the assessment of the different types of tender, i.e. whether it is open, selected or negotiated. The shortcomings of the former have been discussed, and the natural reaction is to devise some procedure to ensure that bids bear some resemblance to the cost of the work to be executed. In countries where no schedule of rates has been developed by the client this is somewhat difficult, as they themselves often do not have a clear idea of the actual cost of the job. One strange system previously adopted in the Islamic Republic of Iran[16] was to discard the highest and lowest figure, average them out and take the one which was closest to the client's estimate. This seems to have no rational basis and invalidates the whole point of tendering. Another system, used in Nepal,[17] when contractors' estimates are more than 10 per cent over the client's, is to call in the three lowest bidders and negotiate for the lowest bid. Depending on the state of the market for contractors, this could also lead to some undesirable results.

Given the irrationality of the implementation of open tendering, many clients resort to selected tendering, i.e. choosing a group of contractors of known experience and viability and putting the tender out to this small group. From the purely financial point of view this probably leads to a more realistic tender. However, it must be said that this automatically means, in the public sector at least, that public money is being used to sponsor a small group of entrepreneurs, and a decision has to be taken as to whether this is acceptable.

Negotiated contracts are usually used for specialized work and the tender is usually based on a cost-plus-percentage basis. Thus a basic cost for doing the work is agreed upon, the contractor puts a percentage on for his overheads and profit, and additional payments or penalties are often set against target completion dates. We have already noted the variation on this theme used in the Republic of Korea where the reward for working effectively is a measure of continuity of work.

Bidding Procedures

Once it has been decided whether to send the tender to a selected group based on a classification system, or to have 'blind auction', i.e. any contractor or would-be contractor may submit a bid, it is the turn of the contractor to decide whether to participate and, if he decides to do so, to prepare his tender submission. For a well-established contractor the mechanics of this process are not a problem. Local contractors with relatively little experience, however, often have difficulties at this stage. They may be perfectly capable of executing the work but, given the nature of construction financing, it is the tender document which will govern: (a) whether they win the contract; and (b) the way in which the contract is financed. Most small contractors do not command the financial management skills which are required to minimize the risks inherent in the tendering system. The early stages of work that a contractor does have to be self-financed, for he receives payment only after, and often a long time after, interim payment stages have passed (although 'mobilization advances' are available in some countries).

In submitting a tender for a contract it should be recognized that the only part of that contract that a contractor has any say in is the financial one. In general, the framework or conditions of contract are laid down. The conditions are generally written to transfer as much responsibility as possible to the contractor. In the developed countries, this is usually accepted, as the contractor has sufficient experience and financial and managerial expertise to be able to deal with this responsibility. Most neophyte domestic contractors in developing countries are not so lucky.

The conditions of contract are usually based on those pertaining in the developed world: 'FIDIC' for civil engineering works; and, for English-speaking countries, the 'RIBA' form of contract for building. However, the responsibility and restrictions are often even more loaded against the contractor in developing countries.

In a survey of the use of their conditions of contract in 50 countries, FIDIC[18] noted that:

(i) The conditions were widely used.
(ii) Whilst the conditions provide for a 10 per cent performance bond (clause 10) it is frequently increased to 20-25 or, exceptionally, 100 per cent.
(iii) Adverse weather conditions are sometimes deemed to be the responsibility of the contractor.
(iv) Clause 20, which deals with excepted risks which do not have to be borne by the contractor, is often deleted.

It is interesting to note that the World Bank team suggested,[19] not an increase of the responsibility placed upon the contractor, as seems to be the case as indicated by the FIDIC survey, but that in the initial stages of development:

(i) The client should accept responsibility for damage to the works caused by natural causes, thus avoiding the need for a contractor to take out insurance.
(ii) The client should take responsibility for carrying out and guaranteeing sub-surface conditions.
(iii) The contractor should be relieved of the responsibility of advising the client of deficiencies in the drawings.
(iv) Penalties for late completion should be small; and even
(v) The contractor should be relieved of responsibility for non-wilful negligence.

Thus, on the one hand, there is the World Bank study which recommended a paternalistic, supportive approach to local contractors and, on the other, the reality of conditions of contract being

Table 5 Aspects of the tendering system.

Country	Performance bond	Bid guarantee	Advance	Bank credit facilities	Retention	Penalty clause
Bangladesh[1]	high	12.5%		100% collateral, poor		
Nepal[2]	5%			Up to 100% collateral, poor	5%	
Niger[3]		5% non-reimbursable	15%			100%
Ghana[4]			20%	poor	5%	
Philippines[5]	30%	5%			10%	
Swaziland[6]	10%			100% collateral		
Republic of Korea[7]	10%	10%	up to 30% cooperative	poor, 30–40% interest rate	5%	
Iran[7]	5%			good	10%	
Ethiopia[7]	15%	5%		fair	10%	
Sri Lanka[8]	2.5%	2.5%	20%	poor, 30% interest rate	5%	.025% per day

Sources: [1] World Bank, *Bangladesh—a Review of the Construction Industry* (Washington, 1978).
[2] Idem, *Nepal—A Review of the Construction Industry* (February 1978).
[3] B. Balkenhol, *Small Contractors: Untapped Potential or Economic Impediment?* (Geneva, ILO, 1979; mimeographed World Employment Programme research working paper; restricted).
[4] G. Ofori, *The Construction Industry in Ghana* (Geneva, ILO, December 1981; mimeographed World Employment Programme research working paper; restricted).
[5] FIDIC, *Inquiry into Use of Conditions of Contract (International) for Works of Civil Engineering Construction* (1973).
[6] UNIDO, *Kingdom of Swaziland—The Construction Industry Survey and Identification Report* (Report No. 5, January 1979).
[7] World Bank, *A Framework for the Promotion of Construction Industries in the Developing Countries* (Staff Working Paper No. 168, November 1973).
[8] S. Ganesan, *The Construction Industry in Sri Lanka* (Geneva, ILO, February 1982; mimeographed World Employment Programme Research Working Paper; restricted).

modified to increase the constraints laid upon contractors. An indication of the variation in various aspects of tendering is shown in Table 5.

Before actually submitting a tender, a contractor has to prepare it. Having decided, or having been asked, to tender he will receive various documents—the conditions of contract, the specification and the bill of quantities. The conditions of contract are discussed above. There would seem to be an *a priori* case for simplified conditions of contract, particularly in relation to small contractors with limited experience. This is not merely because the conditions are often too onerous for small contractors, or that some of the conditions are not enforceable.[20] It is basically because the level of sophistication of both the contractor and the works entrusted to him do not justify such sophisticated conditions of contract.

The bill of quantities from which a contractor prepares his tender bid is, to the uninitiated, a strange and forbidding document. It splits up a project in such a way that its elements can be counted and separately priced, but bears very little relation to the way in which a contractor would actually go about doing the work. Thus it is a creation that appeals to the sensibilities of accountants, economists and quantity surveyors, but which is of marginal utility to the people at the end of the chain of command who have to put the structure together.

The procedure for preparing a bill of quantities has a certain mathematical elegance as the project is divided neatly into trades, then into individual items, and laid out on the various pages with a description of each number item on the left, followed by the quantity in linear metres, square metres, cubic metres or just plain numbers. Then two columns are left blank for the contractor to fill in; his unit price and the full price for the item (quantity × unit price). Having exercised his arithmetical skills at multiplication the contractor is then expected to try his hand at addition by bringing forward the total money sums for each page as totals for each bill (i.e. each trade, plus 'preliminaries'), and the grand total plus a percentage addition for contingencies makes up the contractor's tender.

The essential trouble with the bill of quantities, from the contractor's point of view, is that there is just so much of it. A bill for a comparatively small project may run to several hundred pages, and the estimating process—if done properly—is both time-consuming and expensive (particularly if an outside quantity surveyor has to be employed). Worse still, the bidder has to pay for the privilege of getting the contract documents, and his whole investment in bid preparation will be lost unless his bid is successful. Thus every invitation to tender prevents a contractor with a dilemma; he can either prepare a thorough bid with painstaking care (and risk losing the substantial consequent investment of time and money) or gamble on a quick 'guesstimate' which, if 'successful', could be much lower than the eventual cost and leave him with a much more serious loss.

Thorough preparation of an estimate based on a bill of quantities demands considerable skills in numerical manipulation as well as a good grasp of materials and other costs. In order to produce an accurate estimate, each of several hundred items must be broken down into its elements of materials, labour, plant and overheads. Thus the cost estimate for a cubic metre of mass concrete will typically have to be assembled from separate estimates of the costs of the appropriate quantities of all the elements.

The idea of calculating a price for just 1 m^3 of concrete is somewhat artificial, since the optimum method of batching, mixing, transporting, compacting and curing will all depend very much on the quantity, rate of placing and structural layout. The bidder will gain some impression of the volume of work from the quantity stated against the item, but he will also have to take into account the consumption of the relevant resources in the other items of the bill. Thus, although he may need 100 tonnes of cement on the job as a whole, this may be spread among 30 or 40 separate items. Plant and labour are even more difficult to estimate, as a concrete mixer, dumper or gang of labourers may contribute in a small way to three-quarters of the bill items, but their costs have to be recovered bit by bit from each one. Overheads are yet more difficult to allocate, and most bidders do this on an arbitrary percentage basis.

The cubic metre of concrete may be destined for a retaining wall, in which case there will be other items for excavation, shuttering and steelfixing. Confusingly for the bidder, these will appear in different bills entitled 'groundworks', 'carpentry' and 'steel-fixing.' Thus a technically-proficient contractor, with a good idea of the resources that will be required for that portion of the project, will only be able to check his estimate by drawing out a series of items distributed almost randomly through the various trade bills. In the experience of the authors, this is simply beyond the skills of most small-/medium-sized developing country contractors (plus a good many in industrialized countries as well!).

The structure of items for trench excavation is particularly artificial. Any sensible contractor asked to excavate a trench 4 metres deep from A to B would start at one end and work his way steadily to the other. Not so the quantity surveyor. He will start with an item for 'excavation up to 2 metres deep', then remove (on paper) another layer 'more than 2 metres and up to 3 metres' and follow up with a final layer 'more than 3 metres and up to 4 metres.' Admittedly this approach is not without its advantages, as the separation of items for various depths allows the contractor to recover his inevitably higher costs in undertaking deeper excavation, while the same group of items can be used to determine prices for a number of trenches. For an experienced and numerate contractor the fact that the method of calculation is at variance with the method of executing the work is no more than a minor irritation. For the typical practical developing country contractor with a limited educational background, however, the dichotomy in methods presents a definite barrier to understanding. This puts him at a clear disadvantage in relating his bid prices to his practical experience of physically executing similar works in the past.

Thus for the average contractor, the only feasible way of preparing a bid is to start by calculating the cost of carrying out the work in the way that he plans to do it, working out the overall cost of materials, labour, plant and overheads. He may then be confident of his price for the project as a whole, but a major mathematical task lies ahead of him in satisfying the esoteric demands of the quantity surveyor.

He does this by disaggregating the overall figure and distributing it among the various bill items in such a way that (hopefully) he will not lose if the quantities are changed later. Indeed the really shrewd bidder will try to outguess the designer by inflating unit prices for those items where he believes quantities will rise (e.g. "extra over for excavation in rock" with a nominal quantity, at a site where he believes a thick layer of rock underlies the surface) while trimming them where there is a good chance of a reduction. A further refinement is to boost cash flow by loading the items that will be measured early against the later items like internal finishes. These guessing games can be very profitable, but they can also be hazardous for the bidder whose manipulative skills are not of a high order.

The main advantage of the conventional bill of quantities remains its flexibility in that, by remeasurement at the conclusion of the works using the contractor's unit prices, any design changes can be easily accommodated (it also allows comparison of key unit prices from contract to contract). It can therefore be seen as an insurance against the client's (and his professional advisers') lack of initial diligence, since they can throw together a set of indicative contract drawings in the knowledge that errors, omissions and changes of mind can be dealt with by working drawings and amendments.

It is therefore a system which confers apparent benefits on the client, the designer and the quantity surveyor, while creating a mass of unwanted clerical work for the overburdened, relatively innumerate and probably unremunerated bidder. The bidder, of course, has to play the game according to rules set by others (or not play at all). Thoughtful clients might, on the other hand, wonder whether the apparent benefits are also real. By putting a premium on financial rather than technical skills, and by placing the bidder in a clear adversarial relationship from the start, the client cuts himself off from a source of valuable practical advice. Instead he makes it likely that he will end up with a wily opponent, whose primary objectives are commercial rather than technical. We believe that some compromise should be possible, leading to a rationalization and simplification of the more esoteric aspects of the quantity surveyor's craft while maintaining adequate protection for the client, and in Chapter 5 we outline a possible approach towards meeting this aim.

Contract financing

In preparing a price for the contract one would imagine that the contractor would first plan how he would carry out the work, then put a price to this plan and enter the figures in the bill. This, however, ignores the fact that a contractor's major financial problem is not just the amount of money he will eventually receive but also the *timing* of those receipts. As we shall see, the contractor has to make a heavy initial outlay in bonds, insurance, purchase of materials and costs of setting up his site. To remain financially solvent he needs to minimise the gap between cumulative expenditure and income. Unfortunately, he would normally get paid very little at the beginning of a contract because: (a) work is only just starting; and (b) the initial works are relatively minor as regards cost. We have already referred to the predilection among experienced and shrewd contractors to 'load' the items that are likely to be measured early in the contract as a means of boosting cash flow, which effectively rewards financial expertise as against technical skills.

It should be remembered that the contractor, in theory, makes a reasonable profit by maximizing the use of his available resources. His end product is clearly defined and it is therefore only in the manner of achieving this end product that he can make money. In practice, however, the experienced contractor takes advantage of the possibility of manipulating the bill of quantities to optimize his cash flow situation.

Generally tenders are adjudicated on a least-cost basis. Where experienced contractors are tendering for a job, this approach would normally be effective in identifying the contractor who can effectively execute the work at the least cost. Moreover, most clients (whether public or private) in developed countries have their own schedule of rates and can therefore readily arrive at a reasonable estimate of a tender price against which contractors' bids can be compared, so a bid which is markedly lower than the estimate would be analysed in detail and probably rejected. In a situation, however, where one is dealing with inexperienced contractors and where there is no schedule of rates, as in most developing countries, there is a serious danger that the lowest bidder will be totally incapable of executing the work for that price. Moreover, many small contractors allow hope to triumph over experience in putting in a tender which is extremely low to ensure that they obtain work.

Nevertheless, let us assume that the small contractor has managed to price his bill of quantities (or has obtained the services of one who will do it for him) and has arrived at a price which he feels is reasonable and provides him with monthly payments which will allow him to operate financially. He must then submit the bid to the client.

Because contracting is a risky, albeit occasionally highly lucrative, occupation most clients wish to ensure that the bid is a serious one. They will therefore demand that each bid is accompanied by a guarantee which can be as high as $12\frac{1}{2}$ per cent of the contract sum (as in Bangladesh)[21] or, more commonly, 5 per cent (Ethiopia,[22] Philippines,[23] Niger[24]) and may be reimbursable or not (as in Niger[24]). Small contractors frequently experience difficulty in negotiating bank guarantees to cover bid bonds, and the alternative of providing a cash deposit can severely deplete their liquid resources.

In addition, the validity of the bid is often circumscribed by the client. In Nepal,[25] for example, the validity is specified as 90 days or 'any extended reasonable period required by the employer'. Given the convoluted administrative procedures often involved in awarding a contract, the validity may be grossly extended and in countries with high rates of inflation this may automatically make a potentially profitable bid into a certain financial disaster.

Any discussion of contract financing tends to ignore politely an issue which plays a significant role in the construction industry. Because of its split of responsibility and the concentration in the hands of a few regarding the awarding and monitoring of contracts, the scope for corruption is fairly broad. Whilst it is a sensitive area, it is of little value pretending that it does not exist. Indeed some contractors would consider it a fact of life. Its existence reinforces the argument that a contractor's skill tends to be most revered in the financial rather than the technical sphere.

Executing the Job – and Getting Paid!

The enterprising contractor may perhaps be excused for heaving a sigh of relief and satisfaction when, the complexities of the tendering process surmounted, he is actually awarded a contract. For domestic contractors in most developing countries, however, the bidding process merely provides a foretaste of the costs, risks and difficulties that will have to be overcome during the execution of the project. Some of these problems will of course be technical in nature, but they are likely to be dwarfed by the myriad contractual and financial constraints arising from the client's cumbersome, illogical and generally unhelpful administrative procedures.

Before he can even move on to the site, the contractor must negotiate a satisfactory bond and insurance of the works. The performance bond is usually a considerable percentage of the contract sum. In Ethiopia[26] it is 15 per cent, whilst in the Philippines[27] it is as much as 30 per cent. Naturally most small contractors do not have this type of money available, and have to obtain a guarantee from the bank. The latter are naturally suspicious of contractors and often demand 100 per cent collateral on the guarantee in the form of buildings, plant, etc. Thus the debit side of the contractor's cash flow looks distinctly bad even before he starts the job.

Having arranged a performance bond and insurance to the client's satisfaction, the contractor can start thinking about mobilizing his resources of labour, equipment and materials. The cash flow implications of the first two are unlikely to be too serious, as he will probably own an inventory of basic equipment and any additional labour that is recruited can be paid weekly or monthly in arrears. Materials are a more serious problem. Suppliers are generally unwilling to grant credit facilities to domestic contractors, so the contractor must either pay for the initial consignment direct from his own pocket or seek a loan from a bank, a relative or a business associate. This would be bad enough if the contractor, like his industrialized country counterpart, could plan and schedule his orders so that deliveries (and therefore payments) are not made until shortly before the items are to be incorporated into the structure. In fact when, as often happens, the availability of key materials such as cement is irregular and unpredictable, the unfortunate contractor can only ensure orderly progress of his site work by carrying excess stocks. This results in a more onerous cash flow penalty than would otherwise be incurred.

As an example of the problems encountered by contractors, the payment procedure adopted in Ghana is not atypical:

> The large contractors put in a claim, the smaller ones invite the quantity surveyor to the site to undertake a valuation of the work executed. The surveyor, having agreed with the contractor on the value of work done (and therefore the value of the certificate), prepares a certificate for payment. The certificate is signed by the project architect, and then by the regional consultant of the government organization as well as the regional head of the ministry or department which is the client of the project, who applies for funds to be released. The certificate and a progress report, which indicates percentages of the main elements of construction that have been completed, are then sent to the regional economic planning officer.
>
> The economic planning officer visits the site and confirms the validity of the progress report. This is done in connection with his duties of ensuring proper implementation (according to development plans) and keeping track of developments in the region.
>
> The regional administrative officer and the regional commissioner sign the certificate, which is then sent to the capital. There, it goes first to the headquarters of the client ministry or department, where it passes through some bureaucratic procedures, and is then forwarded on to the Ministry of Finance.
>
> At Finance a check is made to see whether the project is listed in

the annual estimates. Several persons look at the certificate. From the scheduling officer it goes to an assistant secretary, to a principal assistant secretary, the director of budgets, the principal secretary, and, finally, the Commissioner. Then it comes back through successively lower officers until it gets to a despatch clerk who hands out a warrant to the contractor. This is the warrant for release of funds, signed by the Commissioner for Finance.

The papers go back to the headquarters of the client ministry or department, and then to the regional office of that ministry where vouchers are prepared for payment. The regional administrative officer signs the financial encumbrance, and the contractor can then collect a cheque from the regional treasury to the value of the certificate.

The length of the government's certification and payment procedures, as well as its centralization in the capital, are dictated by the budgeting process and the government's financial policy. The Regional Commissioner (the government's representative in the region) is not empowered to sign warrants for the release of central government funds. The long process is considered a means of building accountability into the system by having one party checking on the other party's work, and so on. This safeguards the government against overpaying contractors. Officials in the civil service tend to defend the *status quo*, and contractors and professionals tend to criticize it.

The process is clearly cumbersome, and the delays it entails create financial problems for contractors. Moreover, the contractor has to personally (or through his representative) push the certificate along from one stage to the next, including the steps that are executed in the capital. This leads to extra overheads in time lost, travelling costs and hotel bills. The multiplicity of steps, the large number of people involved in them and the personal contact the contractor has with them (to persuade or plead with them) makes the incidence of corruption more likely, involving the contractor in further financial loss.

The length of the payment process depends on the individual contractor. The most serious delays occur when the government runs out of funds; the certificates are held up in the office of the Commissioner for Finance for long periods, to the detriment of contractors, most of whom rely on these interim payments to operate their enterprises, to acquire materials and pay employees' wages.[28]

Whilst the convoluted payment procedures described in the Ghana case study (see Chapter 3 below) are extreme, prompt payment by clients after a regular monthly measurement as specified in the usual contract documents is the exception rather than the rule. Thus it is only a rich contractor who can afford to devote his full attention to the technical and management aspects of running his sites, and long-term planning is a luxury few domestic contractors can afford. The main task must be to keep the cash flow problem within bounds, keeping creditors at bay while relentlessly pursuing debtors, in the hope that eventually a real bankable profit will emerge. The primary attributes for success are therefore pragmatism, patience and perseverance, not to mention an eye for the main chance and good connections in the right places. These qualities (at least the first three) are no doubt admirable, but thoughtful clients might sometimes reflect that they would be better served by contractors who were less commercially sophisticated but more technically proficient.

Having shown the problems which face a contractor in even starting work, it would perhaps be merely piling on the agony to discuss the question of retention money, strict application of the conditions of contract due to the lack of confidence and experience of government/consultant engineers, or the problems of working under fixed-price contract in periods of high inflation. Clearly the system seems to be geared to suppress the small indigenous contractor rather than to assist him.

The question that has to be asked first is whether governments accept that a change is necessary so that small contractors can be allowed to grow. One can certainly argue that any contractor who actually flourishes in these circumstances deserves to do so. However, does he flourish because he is technically and managerially efficient, or because he knows better than others how to circumvent the system? In the following two chapters, we look at the construction industry in two very different political and socio-economic environments—Sri Lanka and Ghana—to demonstrate how the institutional framework constrains (or supports) the industry in practice.

CHAPTER 3
The Case of Ghana*

The story of the construction industry in Ghana over the last decade is, like that of the country itself, one of promise unfulfilled. What we have to discover is the extent to which this was predetermined by the institutional environment. Could construction have stood out as a sector while the remainder of the economy was in decline? Could a better performance by the construction industry have helped to stimulate a general recovery? If the answer to either of these questions could be even a tentative 'yes', we have a chance to test out the thesis put forward in Chapter 2. This is that the transferred framework within which so many construction industries in developing countries have to operate leads directly to institutional constraints, which in turn hold back the development of the domestic sector.

The Industry and the Economy

Ghana is a country that is relatively well-endowed with resources. A hard-working people, significant mineral reserves (including fat veins of gold in Ashanti) and a strong agricultural base, with cocoa still accounting for 60 per cent of commodity exports despite a steady decline in production over the last 20 years. Yet living standards, particularly for the rural poor, have declined significantly from the days when Ghana could confidently claim to be the richest country in black Africa, and it is one of the unfortunate few to have exhibited a negative average annual growth rate (of −2 per cent) in GNP per capita over the last decade. Over the same period inflation has gone from the low teens to an estimated 120–140 per cent, while foreign exchange is desperately short and the cedi (official exchange rate: cedis 2·75 to 1 US dollar) fetched (at the time of writing, 1982) only about one-fifteenth of its official value on the black market.**

---

* This chapter is based on the work of George Ofori and in particular, 'The construction industry in Ghana', mimeographed *World Employment Research Working Paper*, restricted (Geneva, ILO, December 1980).
**The cedi was devalued by 90% against the US dollar in October 1983.

Ghana has had a number of governments since independence in 1957, and all have put forward (but not always implemented) policies that affect the construction industry. These policies have ranged from passive 'encouragement', through subsidy, assistance and control to active participation through direct labour units or parastatals.

A very wide range of technologies have been used in Ghana, from the most modern and sophisticated to the most basic and simple. Whilst this can be viewed as a sensibly pragmatic response to different needs and criteria, there is also sometimes a suspicion of confusion. For example, while the government was still showing interest in industrialized housing systems, the 1975-80 Plan stated:[1]

> Government will make the greatest use of the skills already acquired by the rural people to build houses for themselves by providing technical assistance through the Department of Rural Development.

The policy regarding public or private sector execution of construction projects has been equally unclear, with emphasis sometimes tilting towards encouragement of private sector consultants and contractors, while at other times the policy has been to build up public sector capacity.

It is fair to note that many government initiatives over the last twenty years have been directed towards encouraging local control over the industry, and this is perhaps more important than defining a clear boundary between the responsibilities of the public and private sectors. Thus the objective in setting up the State Construction Corporation in 1966 was to provide a purely Ghanaian construction organization which could compete effectively with the foreign firms that dominated the market for larger and more technically complex public works projects. Equally, the Bank for Housing and Construction was set up in 1973 with, as one of its major functions, the task of providing loans to prefinance projects to be undertaken by domestic contractors.

Overall construction output at 1980 prices is estimated to be of the order of 500 million cedis (or US$180 million at the official exchange rate). Construction output per capita has fluctuated wildly in recent years. From a level of 29 cedis in 1965 it declined to 16 cedis three years later, increased to 26 cedis in 1971, 43 cedis in 1974 and 46 cedis in 1980. Bearing in mind the accelerating rate of inflation, the overall trend is of course strongly downwards.

Fluctuating and declining demand is inevitably discouraging to potential providers of construction capacity, and realistic contractors and materials suppliers have learned to take official demand forecasts set out in development plans with a large dose of scepticism. For example in 1965 (just before the sharp drop in output per capita), a report on the first year of the Seven Year Development Plan stated:[3]

> In this financial year 1965 we must catch up with our construction and production timetables for all major enterprises and for the educational programme.

This was at a time when materials and other key inputs were available. The difficulties then were with contracting capacity, as numerous development projects had been commissioned all over the country. In 1974, when output had recovered, the government lamented that:[4]

> ... low constructional capacity has led to another situation where projects have remained in the estimates for a long time without being implemented.

The lack of confidence understandably inhibited investment, and foreign exchange restrictions were partly responsible for shortages in equipment for materials manufacture, plant and spare parts. The situation persisted, and the 1978–9 Budget Statement commented:[5]

> Over the years a large number of projects have been started all over the country which have not been completed and are likely to remain on the books for quite some time. While constraints such as input availability have contributed to this situation, it is also becoming clear that most contractors have far too much on their plate, in the sense that the number of contracts awarded them exceeds their capacity.

Construction is a high risk business at the best of times. Even with stable demand and plentiful supplies of skilled manpower, materials and equipment a contractor must stand by his bid assumptions on input cost trends, ground and climatic conditions. Unfortunately, few countries have taken (or, perhaps, been able to take) account of the truth expressed by the Economic Commission for Europe that:[6]

> It has become clear that stable levels of construction activity are a prerequisite for general economic stability as well as for further progress in construction.

In Ghana, as elsewhere, economic planners continued to see contractors as wizards, capable of conjuring men, materials and machinery out of thin air. The reality is unfortunately more mundane. Contractors are mere fallible human beings. Expensive resources can only be built up slowly, and this will only happen if there is a reasonable prospect of them being put to profitable use over a sufficient period to amortize their purchase and running costs. Few planners go on from concocting a construction demand plan to work out a construction capacity plan, backed by policy measures and financial resources to ensure that the two match. Ghana has shown itself to be no exception to this general rule. Because their livelihoods are at stake, contractors have learned to distinguish the wishful-thinking element in economic plans from the harsh reality. Sometimes this is not too difficult. They know that their businesses cannot grow if the nation's economy is at crisis point. Thus the thinking contractor would balance the criticism of his industry quoted earlier from the 1978-9 Budget Statement against the portents suggested by the following statement from the same document:[5]

> The tempo of economic activity, as measured by the Real Gross Domestic Product, has been declining over the period since 1974. The external accounts are grossly out of balance, with the best estimates showing that reserves are at a very low level.

Prior to 1966 construction employment was in excess of 70,000 (72,800 in 1965, representing 18 per cent of all recorded employment). However, almost three-quarters of these jobs were in the public sector, and a dramatic reduction in construction employment occurred in 1966 following a change in government. The Workers' Brigade—a direct labour organization undertaking labour-intensive construction projects throughout the country—was disbanded, other direct labour organizations were pruned down, and the private sector laid off about 5,000 workers as the new government suspended numerous projects. Since then total recorded employment in construction has hovered around 50,000 (10 per cent or so of total recorded employment) and approximately two-thirds of these jobs have been in the public sector.

The accelerating rate of inflation has had a disrupting influence on the industry, and cost planning has become an increasingly hazardous exercise for both contractors and their clients. It is estimated that over the decade 1970-9 alone average building costs per square metre rose by about 2,000 per cent (from 0·35 cedis to 10 cedis). The shares of the various factors of production in building costs are currently estimated to be:

Materials	50–55 per cent
Labour	20–25 per cent
Plant	0– 5 per cent
Profits and overheads	15–25 per cent

The low share of plant costs is attributable to the labour-intensive nature of most building projects in Ghana. The apparently high share of profits and overheads reflects the increasing operational problems faced by contractors. Shortages of skilled labour, materials, plant and spare parts are commonplace, and delays in honouring certified payments, especially by public sector clients, are a severe burden for the undercapitalized contractor. Faced with this rising tide of uncertainties, contractors have reacted by boosting their bid prices to protect their position. In this they have been only partially successful, as they lose both time and money lobbying for contracts, seeking out scarce materials, chasing certificates and the payments that should automatically follow, whilst site productivity dwindles due to delayed deliveries and plant breakdowns.

Administration

For a country of 11 million or so inhabitants, successive Ghanaian governments have contrived a remarkably complex administrative system, in which the construction industry has often found itself enmeshed. This administrative structure still bears a resemblance to that of the United Kingdom, from which it was borrowed. But there is a general feeling among practical builders that the British taste for bureaucracy has, with a number of honourable exceptions, been developed to an excruciating level of refinement. The situation is not improved when politicians, impatient with the slow grind of conventional procedures, disregard professional advice and take precipitate decisions on favourite schemes. The problem is not confined to the construction industry. And it has at least been recognized. A responsible public official recently asked:[7]

> What public institution in Ghana can claim to have escaped the indiscipline, lack of procedure and wanton abuse of public trust which has characterized our economic life in the past few years?

Unfortunately bureaucracy begets bureaucracy. To tackle the problem of corruption, government has had to assign other individuals or organizations to oversee existing administrators, particularly where finance is involved. In the construction industry this has resulted in a very long process of certifying payments due to the contractor, with numerous checks and counter-checks, so that contract receipts can be months or even years in arrears.

Overall responsibility for the health, wealth and growth of the Ghanaian construction industry rests with the Ministry of Works and Housing, which is also the parent body for a number of construction parastatals. The Ministry is highly centralized, and all important decisions are made in Accra. Its activities in the regions and districts have been delegated to the subordinate Public Works Department, which has itself experienced an eventful series of reorganizations since it was inherited from the colonial administration. The Department was originally responsible for initiating, designing and administering all public projects, as well as constructing most of them by direct labour. Soon after independence it was renamed the Ghana National Construction Corporation (GNCC) and given prime responsibility for implementing the ambitious public investment plans of the new government.

The GNCC lasted until 1966, when it was split in two under a decree of the new military regime. As a result, the Public Works Department (PWD) re-emerged with responsibility for 'consultancy and planning of new developments and maintenance of existing facilities', leaving a State Construction Corporation (SCC) to concentrate on the physical execution of projects.

A year later, a further reorganization took place. Responsibility for roads was split off into a Ghana Highway Authority (GHA), while design and management of other major projects was transferred to a new Architectural and Engineering Services Corporation (AESC). To complicate matters further, the PWD Hydraulics Division was merged with the Department of Rural Water Development to form the Water Supplies Division. This was incorporated into the Ghana Water and Sewerage Corporation. The remaining rump of the PWD has an important residual role in registration of private contractors and consultants, vetting designs submitted by public sector clients, planning and design of minor works and maintenance of a wide variety of public buildings and structures, besides acting as regional representatives of the parent ministry through its network of local offices.

The Ghana Highways Authority was taxed with the formidable task of expanding, improving and maintaining the crumbling network of all-weather roads against the background of a rapidly deteriorating national economic environment. Its responsibilities extend to planning, design and supervision of new works executed by contractors, while it employs a direct labour force of more than 10,000 workers to cope with routine repairs and maintenance. Whilst the Authority set about its task in a workmanlike way, it has been at the mercy of financial and administrative constraints outside its control. It is not remunerated on a fee basis, so must rely upon being allocated a satisfactory share of the Ministry vote. Neither does it control the funds used to finance work done by contractors and external consultants. These funds are held by the Ministry of Finance, and disbursement to the payee, even after issue of the GHA's certificate, has proved extraordinarily cumbersome and time-consuming. Although in theory the GHA has jurisdiction over most trunk and feeder roads, some urban roads are controlled by city and district councils while certain feeder roads are dealt with by the Ghana Cocoa Marketing Board. The lack of clear demarcation can result in either neglect or, in one notable case, the re-award of a contract for an already completed road by another organization!

The Architectural and Engineering Services Corporation was meant to take on all public sector consultancy work and to compete for jobs in the private sector, and it was stated that its services 'were not meant only for development projects in Ghana but also eventually for projects in sister African countries where shortages of skilled manpower become obstacles in the implementation of development projects." In fact shortages of skilled manpower have hit the AESC itself, as its salary levels for professional staff have lagged behind those offered by competing private consultants in Ghana, and other staff have been attracted away to work directly in neighbouring countries. Thus the actual performance of the AESC has been disappointing. It has been forced to pass many projects on to private consultants on its register, reducing its role to that of middleman. Noting this tendency, certain quasi-government institutions like the Social Security and National Insurance Trust, the Ghana Commercial Bank, the State Insurance Company, the universities and the Cocoa Marketing Board retain their own private consultants directly. The AESC was established as a self-supporting, profit-making concern charging commercial fees for its services.

Unfortunately, like many such statutory corporations, it has found that it is easier to charge fees than to recover them. As early as 1977 the Chief Executive commented sadly:[8]

> Our earnings . . . remain largely paper earnings. Much of our fees are yet to be settled by some government departments. Presently clients owe us to the tune of about 6 million cedis.

Worse news was to come. By 1978 outstanding debts had doubled to 12 million cedis. They increased further to 18 million cedis the following year.

The State Construction Corporation (SCC) was set up as an integrated commercial construction enterprise producing its own components and some materials, and undertaking projects all over Ghana as well as outside the country. The remit granted to it in 1966 by Legislative Instrument No. 521 allowed it to:

> . . . undertake, plan, carry out, construct, execute, improve, administer and manage, both in Ghana and elsewhere, all kinds of construction projects and civil works, whether public or private or otherwise, including roads, railways, bridges and harbours; . . . works of irrigation, reclamation . . . ; to install electric and telephone appliances and similar things on . . . buildings; to manufacture, . . . or in any manner transform clay, wood, stone, marble, cement, ornamental products . . .

A key consideration in setting up the SCC was the need to increase indigenous control over the industry as there were no private domestic contractors capable of competing with foreign firms for sizeable projects. It was also felt that the prospect of competition from the SCC would have the effect of moderating bid prices by breaking the effective oligopoly enjoyed by the large foreign firms. Over the years the SCC has put up some of Ghana's most sophisticated and imposing structures and highways. It has coped well with emergency jobs, such as the completion (ahead of a very tight schedule) of runway resurfacing at the Kotoka International Airport in Accra. Indeed it has even succeeded in obtaining and completing (in joint venture) an international contract: a road from Lomé to Lama Kara in Togo. The SCC does about 60 per cent of all public projects in Ghana, and all its contracts are obtained through competitive tender. It enjoys no special preference in contract awards, allocation of materials or honouring of payment certificates.

Indeed it is handicapped by being called upon to take on jobs in remote areas where private contractors are unwilling to work, as well as emergency jobs which may interrupt its planned work schedules. Furthermore, as a public corporation it is not allowed to lay off workers during slack periods, and at times as much as one-third of its work force of 13,000 have been effectively redundant.

The SCC has a head office in Accra and branches in each of the nine regions. It is comprehensively equipped, with its own quarries, joinery workshops, precasting yard, central materials store and plant pool. Although its achievements are creditable, its general operational and financial performance leaves something to be desired. It has been the subject of much (often ill-informed) public criticism for delaying jobs. More seriously, up to the major reorganization exercise mounted in 1976 it had an unbroken record of annual financial losses. The SCC's effective competitors in both building and civil engineering works are the expatriate firms and the few large Ghanaian firms with skilled and experienced managers. To its credit it recognizes the benefits of competition against which its performance can be measured, and it has not advocated the nationalization, or even forced indigenization, of the construction industry.

The State Housing Corporation (SHC) is another significant construction parastatal. It was established by Legislative Instrument No. 415 of 1965 to replace the previous Ghana Housing Corporation. It builds houses throughout the country for rental or sale, with an increasing emphasis on the latter in recent years. It has managed to complete about 5,000 houses over the last decade, of which about half are in Accra, bringing its total housing stock to over 20,000. The SHC employs more than 5,000 people directly, but contracts out larger projects to local firms. Like the other construction parastatals it suffers from input cost problems, exacerbated in its case by the refusal of the Prices and Incomes Board to authorize a compensating increase in rents and sale prices. This is serious for an authority which depends wholly on direct income, supplemented by revolving loans bearing interest at the commercial rate. The only financial assistance provided by the government is a modest infrastructure subsidy, which usually falls well short of requirements. For example, in 1976–7 the SHC estimated that it would require 7·7 million cedis to construct roads and drains. The actual allocation was a mere 0·5 million cedis. The SHC's problems do not end when a housing estate is completed, since it then has to commission (and pay) the Electricity and Water and Sewerage Corporations to provide services to the new units. Since the development programmes of the three Corporations are not co-ordinated, and the SHC is in severe financial difficulties, there are several estates in the country which are completed but which are yet to be supplied with service facilities.

The remaining parastatals and autonomous units reporting to the parent Ministry of Works and Housing are the Ghana Water and Sewerage Corporation, the Tema Development Corporation, the Town and Country Planning Department, Prefabricated Concrete Products Limited and the Rent Control Unit, whose functions are self-explanatory. Thus the Ministry has the unenviable task of supervising the activities of no less than ten separate construction-related organizations within the broad framework of government policy, in addition to its overall responsibility for the management of the construction industry and its long-term development. The former task has inevitably been so time-consuming that proposals to deal with the latter responsibility have languished at the back of the 'pending' file. The frequent reorganizations of the parastatals have added to the problems. Any such exercise in reorganization or division is bound to generate some degree of administrative confusion, lack of clearly defined boundaries between areas of responsibility, inter-organisation rivalry and an adverse affect on the morale of the staff. Thus the task of co-ordinating and integrating the welter of conflicting activities and programmes generated by the new units has been extremely onerous.

Although the Ministry of Works and Housing has overall responsibility for construction, most other organs of government interact with the industry as clients, paymasters, financiers, suppliers or regulators of its activities. Each interface contributes a little more friction to the efficient running of the mechanism, so we need to examine the nature of these interactions and the scope for making the pattern of transactions between the industry and the government less costly in time and resources.

Pricing Policies and Government Regulations

Since money is at the root of most construction problems in Ghana, the Ministry of Finance has a crucial influence on the performance of the industry. To start with, it keeps a tight grip on all government expenditure. All payment certificates on construction contracts have to pass through the Ministry's office in Accra before payment can be effected. If the unfortunate contractor awaiting payment then seeks to borrow, he encounters the effects of the Ministry's control over credit policy and interest rates. Finally, the Ministry has a decisive influence over the availability of new work, through its advice to government on the nature, spread and overall cost of public sector development projects.

The Ministry of Economic Planning's prime responsibility is to draw up and monitor development plans, thereby determining the longer-term prospects for public construction demand. The Ministry's External Aid Division co-ordinates all requests for foreign aid and technical assistance, which influences both construction industry demand and resources. A further significant section is the Implementation Unit, which was set up in the hope of improving on the previous low levels of development project implementation.

Although the prospects of improving feedback into the planning process held some attractions, the effect was to introduce yet another bureaucratic step into the already cumbersome contract payments procedure. The procedure is that officers of the Ministry have to confirm by actual physical inspection the stage of construction shown on interim payment certificates before the regional commissioners sign them. The effect is to put economic planning officers (who have no training in construction) into supervisory positions over professional construction consultants.

The Ministry of Trade and Tourism, through the Department of Commerce, controls the issue of import licenses. Since a high proportion of tools and materials for modern construction, and all construction plant and equipment, are imported, the difficulty in securing import licenses severely constrains the competitiveness of local firms. Input costs are also affected by the Ministry's Internal Trade Section, which supervises the distribution of materials and components and controls their prices. Price control is enforced by price inspectors and the police, guided by current price lists published by the Prices and Incomes Board. The Board itself was established by government decree in 1972, to combine the resources of three bodies: the Incomes Commission, the Public Services Advisory Board and the Pay Research Unit. In fact the general verdict is that price control has not been very effective. Few offenders have been arrested and prosecuted. Some have turned the situation to their advantage. Goods are hoarded and sold in secret, creating artificial shortages and pushing up prices still further. Again, the ineffectiveness of direct control over prices led the government to add further controls over the whole system of distribution. Once again the operators were ahead of the game, covering their tracks by passing goods through a complex chain of middlemen before they reached the final consumer. Mark-ups from 'controlled prices' to black market prices were spectacular. In 1979 a local newspaper pointed out:[9]

> The control price of cement is 13·80 cedis per bag, but it is common knowledge that dealers . . . sell cement at between 50 and 60 cedis per bag.

The effect of building material price controls is to entrap the unwary contractor in a Catch 22 syndrome. Apart from goods sold by the government's accredited distribution agencies (which are in fact quite insufficient), nothing sells in the market at the controlled price. But basic price lists inserted in contract documents are these theoretical controlled prices. Seeking a way out, the contractor looks to the price fluctuation clause in the conditions of contract. Here it states that he can only claim compensation for increased costs on production of relevant invoices and receipts. But issuing invoices or receipts for goods at above the controlled prices would render the seller liable to prosecution, so that escape route too is closed. Only three avenues remain open. Firstly, not buy the materials at all and abandon the job. Secondly, buy the materials and try to convince the client's consultants to find some way of reimbursing the extra cost. Thirdly, least appealing of all, 'write it off to experience' and bear the extra cost themselves (remembering to substantially increase their allowance for contingencies in future estimates).

The Ministry of Labour, Social Welfare and Co-operatives enforces labour and industrial relations legislation and is, through the Department of Co-operatives, responsible for the development, supervision and extension of co-operative activities. The government's policy on industrial relations is based on the principles outlined in ILO Conventions Nos. 87 and 98 concerning freedom of association and protection of the right to organize and bargain collectively. The Standard Conditions of Contract require contractors to pay wages at rates at least equivalent to those paid by the government, but skilled workers can normally command a premium. A more onerous requirement, in view of the ups and downs of the construction business, was introduced by the government in 1972 in the form of:[9]

> ... an order forbidding employers to lay off any number of workers for any reason whatsoever without the written permission of the Commissioner for Labour, Social Welfare and Co-operatives.

Although the order remains on the statute book it has not been enforced in the private sector in recent years, due to the mounting recession. However, it still applies to public corporations such as the State Construction Corporation. As a result the competitiveness of these corporations declines still further, as their financial performance crumples under a deadweight of redundant labour, with the corresponding costs, not only in direct wages but also the overheads of transportation, head office staff and supervision. There is a strong co-operative tradition in Ghana, particularly in the rural areas, and several of the more substantial builders' co-operatives have received assistance from the Department of Co-operatives. Among the more successful examples are the Brong Ahafo Builders' Co-operative, which has completed a number of sizeable projects, and the Builders' Society at Tema which constructs houses for the Tema Co-operative Housing Society.

The Ministry of Industries has absolute authority over new industrial investment in both the public and the private sector. Under the Manufacturing Industries Act (1971) the establishment of any new manufacturing industry, or expansion of an existing industry, can be undertaken only after approval by the Commissioner for Industries. The activities of the Ministry regarding building materials and components investments have important implications for the construction industry as a whole, since these inputs account for more than half of construction costs. The intrinsic scope for local investment in building materials production would appear to be considerable, since the 1975–80 Development Plan estimated that 'about 60 per cent of the building materials are imported every year both directly and indirectly as inputs.' Clearly, it makes little sense to invest in new capacity when there is insufficient foreign exchange to meet their running needs for spare parts and essential raw materials inputs. In 1978 the government admitted:[10]

> ... the foreign exchange situation of the country has imposed unavoidable limitations on the ability of these establishments to produce at any appreciable level of capacity. In fact a large number of these enterprises are only operating at an average level

of 30 per cent of capacity, thus locking up valuable assets that could otherwise be productively utilised.

The Ghana Industrial Holding Corporation (GIHOC), which was established in 1968 to take over existing state interests in various (loss-making) manufacturing corporations, is a dominant force in building materials production. The 20 divisions that came together within the GIHOC umbrella were an unenviable inheritance, with joint accumulated losses amounting to some 15 million cedis. The factors identified as being to blame for this state of affairs were:[11]

(i) Poor location, due to political influence outweighing economic considerations in decisions on siting the units.
(ii) Poor design and obsolete plant, leading to low productivity and inadequate quality control.
(iii) Political patronage in staff appointments, leading to poor management and slack discipline.
(iv) Inadequate working capital, leading to cash flow crises, delayed wage and salary payments and poor morale.
(v) Poor reputation, so that efficient management and technical personnel could not be attracted and financial institutions were reluctant to provide assistance.
(vi) Inadequate financial control, leading to a plethora of bad debts.

It is hard to imagine a less promising scenario. Yet the new GIHOC managers rapidly identified the problems and set about solving them through consolidation and rationalization of product lines, installation of tight financial and credit control systems coupled with a much more realistic approach to planning and general management control. The result was a return to profitability, which is being followed up with an extensive expansion and rehabilitation exercise mounted with assistance from UNDP. As a result of the rationalization GIHOC now has 16 divisions, two subsidiaries and shares in four other industrial concerns. Of these, five produce construction materials:

(i) Brick and Tile Division in Accra.
(ii) Paints Division at Tema.
(iii) Marble Works Division in Accra (terrazzo flooring and marble products).
(iv) Metal Industries, Accra (nails, rivets, etc.).

(v) Steelworks Division at Tema (reinforcement and steel components).

Despite the efforts of GIHOC and the private sector building materials manufacturers, output of key building materials (particularly cement, steel reinforcement and roof sheets) continues to fall well short of even the currently depressed levels of demand. In an attempt to regulate priorities, the government introduced a system of rationing key materials controlled through the regional administrative offices. Although some guidelines as to priority categories are laid down, the procedure is cumbersome and allocations depend on what is available to the region, the discretion of the officials concerned, and (inevitably) the influence wielded by the contractor and his client. In fact some of the more influential public sector clients, such as the Social Security and National Insurance Trust and the State Insurance Corporation, have managed to by-pass the system and import some materials directly. Resulting from the much higher prices obtaining on the black market, a lively 'underground' secondary market in rationed materials has developed with the ultimate distribution in the hands of numerous unidentifiable small retailers who dictate the final selling price. The result is that the reputable manufacturers and merchants are starved of the revenue that could otherwise finance desperately needed new investment, while ballooning building costs are inflated still further.

The Construction Scene

The organization of the construction industry in Ghana, like the framework of contract law and procedures which regulates it, are derived from British practice. Although this organization has been borrowed from the United Kingdom, Ghana has not introduced the more recent changes and refinements that have developed to make the British model work more smoothly. The contractor is never involved in the project at the design stage, package deal contracts have not been tried, and the idea of project management consultancy has not been explored. The same pattern of fragmented organization is applied mechanically to all projects, large and small, and each professional jealously guards his territory at every stage. For example, the quantity surveyor's advice on costs is seldom sought at the design stage, and when his calculations are finally available the design process has gone so far that the architectural consultant is reluctant to backtrack and absorb losses due to abortive work. This compartmentalization runs against a recognition of construction as a process in which the solutions of one sub-group become the tasks of the next, and the most economic and effective result depends on the interaction and interweaving of the inputs of all members of the project team.

The public sector accounts for over 60 per cent of the total demand for modern construction, so the government has potential to dominate the industry in its purchasing role, quite apart from setting the legal and procedural framework and controlling design, execution and materials manufacturing capacity through ministries and parastatals. This potential leadership role is, however, easier to recognize than to realize. For example, the idea of setting up consortia of client organizations which would agree on standard designs to realize economies of scale and eliminate repetitive design work has not been developed. Individual organizations have prepared standard designs for government bungalows, office blocks, school buildings, estate houses, etc., but the scale of standardization has not been sufficient to support the emergence of component manufacturers.

Consultant organization
The consultancy field has been very effectively Ghanaianized. There were very few Ghanaian firms as recently as the 1960s, and most of the Ghanaian professionals worked in the civil service. Now, apart from the AESC and other public sector capacity, there are 30 architectural, 32 engineering and 13 quantity surveying practices on the AESC register alone. With the economy and the construction industry in decline, these firms have done well to survive and establish themselves in a precarious operating environment.

Contractor organization
The history of the development of the contracting industry in Ghana is longer and more complex. Prior to independence the demand for construction was mostly limited to private residential buildings and a few office blocks and bungalows for the government. The private houses were built by the informally organized local 'contractors' who were usually local tradesmen leading a group of workers recruited for the occasion. Public sector contracts were handled by the Public

Works Department and the few expatriate firms that were established in the country. On very large projects, such as harbour construction, bids were solicited from abroad. Soon after independence demand mushroomed as the new government embarked on a massive development programme, building roads, schools, hospitals, office blocks, housing, factories and workshops all over the country. This could have been a tremendous opportunity to develop a domestic contracting industry, but the wherewithal in terms of skilled and experienced construction managers was simply not available. Ghanaians had preferred the older professions of law, medicine, teaching and the ministry, so that there were few qualified local people in the construction professions in the colonial and immediate post-independence years. Those few were mainly in government service and lacked both the motivation and the capital to abandon their hard-won security for the high risk contracting industry. Thus the field was left wide open for additional expatriate firms and those local speculators and businessmen who could afford to try their hand at a diversification from their other commercial interests.

The outcome was that many of the expatriate firms left the country when the boom eased and there were signs that it would become more difficult to repatriate profits. The local firms were unable to take their place, due to the limited technical and managerial skills of their proprietors. In fact competition intensified at the bottom end of the market, as the afterglow of the earlier high profits attracted more and more untried entrepreneurs. Meanwhile, the exodus of many expatriate firms at the top end of the market made life easier for those who remained, and they settled down to enjoy a comfortable oligopoly. It was partly to forestall this development that the government formed the State Construction Corporation to engage in large-scale commercial contracting. (With hind-sight it might have been better advised to have pursued a more gradual strategy of developing the more promising private firms).

Contractors for public works are registered in one of four classes according to speciality (building, roads, civil engineering or sub-contracting) on the basis of:

(i) Numbers and qualifications of staff directly employed.
(ii) Plant and equipment inventory.
(iii) Financial capacity (cash and fixed assets).
(iv) Record of work executed in the immediate past.

The equipment requirement is the most formidable, and to be eligible for registration in the minimum grade (for contracts up to 100,000 cedis) a contractor for 'roads and bridges' has to show ownership of one grader, one roller and two tipper trucks and a contractor for 'general buildings' must show one concrete mixer, one tipper truck and one pick-up. Access to hired equipment is not an acceptable substitute for ownership, and the relatively high equipment requirement seems to have been imposed as a way of compensating for the lack of technical expertise among Ghanaian contractors. It may well have the contrary effect, since it tends to act as a barrier to the qualified and really committed people. In fact the checking and control procedures are seldom fully effective, and the government complained in the 1978-9 Statement that:[5]

> ... with almost every contract award, the contractors concerned approach the import licence authorities for allocation to import equipment, despite the criterion that the qualification for consideration for contract award is the possession of the requisite machinery and equipment.

The requirement to employ a minimum qualified staff establishment is also often more honoured in the breach. The smallest road contractors are supposed to employ a works foreman, a bookkeeper, a surveyor and a mechanic, and to have a permanent office. The same category of building contractor should have at least one artisan and an office. In fact most of these small firms are only 'occasional contractors' and run their businesses either from home or the cab of their pick-up truck, employing perhaps a handful of permanent employees who will be supplemented with casual labour as occasion demands. Few small contractors employ bookkeepers, and most of the rest do not keep any books. In the same 1978-9 Budget Statement the government commented mildly that:[1]

> It has been observed that some contractors undertaking government projects do not keep proper accounts on their operations. It is an offence for a registered company not to maintain the proper books of accounts.

Since the break-up of the old Public Works Department in 1973 the AESC, the Highways Authority and the PWD have maintained separate registers and no comprehensive consolidated list is available. The latest data, as at 31 March 1979, are given in Table 6.

Table 6 Registered contractors as at 31 March 1979.

Classification*	Class I	Class II	Class III	Class IV	Total (firms)
A. AESC					
1. Building	32	79	428	681	1,220
2. Civil works	14	34	63	79	
B. Highways	37	51	143	207	438
C. PWD					
1. Roads	6	20	126	83	
2. Civil works	7	12	54	26	
3. Special building	3	3	11	4	
4. General building	9	46	475	581	

* Class I: > 500,000 cedis
Class II: 300,000–500,000 cedis
Class III: 100,000–300,000 cedis
Class IV: < 100,000 cedis.

It would not be correct to add these figures horizontally because some firms are registered with more than one organization, and even within the same organization (AESC and PWD) in different categories. Only the figures for building contractors with AESC and those for firms with the Highways Authority are reliable totals. These figures represent a substantial growth in numbers of firms registered over the period 1972–9. Considering only the number of road and civil engineering contractors registered with the Highways Authority, the figure of 438 is more than double the total of 181 in the last comprehensive register in 1972. Building contractors (considering AESC only) show an even more dramatic increase from 364 to 1,220. The national origin of contractors is somewhat confusing, since certain originally expatriate firms are now in the hands of the second generation who are technically Ghanaian. Table 7 on page 68 includes such firms within the general 'expatriate' category, and therefore somewhat understates the impressive degree of indigenization that has been achieved:

It should be noted that most of the joint ventures have arisen as a result of deliberate government policy to encourage expatriate firms to make a longer term commitment to the development of the local industry. The usual practice is for the expatriate firm to supply

Table 7   Origin of contractors registered with the Highways Authority and AESC, 1979.

	Class I	Class II	Class III	Class IV
Highway Authority:				
(i) Expatriate	5	1	1	—
(ii) Joint expatriate-Ghanaian	3	—	—	—
(iii) Ghanaian	29	50	142	207
Total	37	51	143	207
AESC:				
(i) Expatriate	9	—	—	—
(ii) Joint expatriate-Ghanaian	2	—	—	—
(iii) Ghanaian	21	79	428	681
Total	32	79	428	681

equipment and technical expertise, while the Ghanaian firm contributes the local component in terms of offices, manpower and goodwill (including contacts). It is as yet too early to assess the success or otherwise of this approach.

Most of the larger firms in categories I and II are competent and reasonably well-equipped. Indeed, when account is taken of the difficult economic and commercial environment in which they operate, their performance is spectacularly good. Many of the smaller firms are much less reliable, with ownership in the hands of people with no knowledge of, or commitment to, the construction industry. In some cases the trading names chosen by the proprietors speak for themselves, ranging from 'trading and construction companies' through 'trading, transport and construction companies' to plain 'traders' or vague 'enterprises.'

One of the most promising developments during the 1970s was the flow of professionally qualified people into the domestic contracting sector, including civil engineers, building technologists and quantity surveyors. In view of their lack of capital, these professionals mostly went into partnership with established businessmen. In general these new firms have made good progress. Some of them, after only a few years trading, are now among the largest and most successful contracting firms in the country. Indeed the State Construction Corporation has stated that, of its eight major competitors, four were expatriate-owned or joint ventures, but no less than four were recently-formed companies owned and managed by professional Ghanaians. The government is anxious to encourage this trend, and has stated its intention of:[12]

> ... encouraging professional personnel to enter the construction industry, while efforts will be made to improve the managerial and technical competence of existing contractors.

Problems
The main problem faced by these professionals is lack of finance. Although mobilization advances of up to 20 per cent of contract value are sometimes made by public sector clients, these advances are hedged around with restrictions (payments to be made direct to suppliers, deeds of assignment of plant to the employer, etc.) and are counterbalanced by later delays in honouring certified interim payments. Builders' merchants and suppliers will only consider credit arrangements for well-established firms, so this potential source of working capital is also closed to the newer contractor. Commercial banks are generally reluctant to provide other than very short term loan and overdraft facilities to domestic contractors, since their lending experience with this high-risk group of customers has been very poor. This leaves the development banks, particularly the Bank for Housing and Construction (BHC). The BHC is one of the few development institutions in Africa (other than the National Construction Corporation of Kenya) to have formulated a programme of lending to meet the working capital needs of domestic contractors. The Bank has been cautious in setting up the scheme in a way that should safeguard its interest. Through its Project Services Department it assesses the general record and resources of the contracting firm as well as the potential profitability of the (public sector) project against which it is proposed to lend. The prospective borrower is then required to agree to open a special project account into which all certified payments will be made, and the client is notified that cheques should be made payable in the joint names of the contractor and the Bank. The Bank then effectively appoints itself the contractor's paymaster for the duration of the project, and examines invoices, payroll sheets etc. before releasing funds from the account. In view of the apparent safeguards the borrowers were not

required to supply collateral under the scheme, although the interest charged on the borrowing was at commercial rates. Foolproof as the scheme must have appeared, it has turned out to be an unhappy experiment for the Bank. Some contractors failed to perform satisfactorily on their projects, so that they either abandoned them or had them terminated by the client. Others managed to secure direct payments from their clients, leaving the Bank without security for its loan. On re-examination, many of the defaulters proved to have overstated their plant and other assets, so legal action to recover the funds would have been pointless. The outcome was a virtual suspension of the Bank's contract financing activities with outstanding doubtful debts amounting to several million cedis.

A further development bank, the Social Security Bank, has been set up by the Social Security and National Insurance Trust and has also embarked on a scheme for contract financing. Whilst the new scheme is based on that operated by the BHC with additional safeguards covering collateral and a more thorough investigation of individual applications, it is too early to assess the lending experience of the new bank.

The BHC has also assisted domestic contractors by setting up a company, Plant Pool Limited, in which it holds a 60 per cent equity interest and which maintains a substantial inventory of heavy plant in Accra, for daily or weekly hire. It also operates a hire purchase scheme, which enables contractors to buy plant, equipment and trucks on deferred terms, and finances quarries and building materials production facilities.

The decree setting up the BHC provided that:[13]

> The bank shall endeavour so far as practicable to develop and promote improvements in building skills of building contractors and to promote efficiency in the construction industry generally.

The BHC has not been able to make much progress in contractor training because its existing facilities were already overstretched and no additional funds were available to finance this activity. The main innovation in contractor training occurred when the World Bank attached a construction management consultant to the BHC to advise its contractor-customers on improved construction management procedures. Since his departure the activity has been continued by the Bank's own engineers, but the impact has been limited in view of the size of the problem and the need to divert their efforts towards attempting to collect overdue loans. On a few occasions, the Bank has assigned some of its qualified personnel to work directly with contractors as agents/site engineers. This must, however, be seen primarily as an attempted rescue programme than as planned on-the-job training.

Other attempts to introduce domestic contractors to construction management training include seminars at the Management Development and Productivity Institute and at the Department for Housing and Planning Research, but they have been poorly attended. Thus the government's expressed intention of 'upgrading the managerial and technical competence of existing contractors' has been tackled only in piecemeal fashion. There has not so far been a fair test of the scope for construction management training in Ghana, since the first step must be to convince the contractor of the gaps in his skills and experience and this should be followed by a properly planned programme to meet the identified training need.

The growth potential of many of the smaller firms in the industry is limited by the highly personalized management style adopted by the proprietors. Perhaps as a result of hard experience, they tend to be highly suspicious and are unwilling to delegate any authority, especially where finance is concerned. As a result they tend to be busy, rather than effective, managers. Constantly on the move, the typical small contractor purchases his own materials, pays his workers, supervises his foremen, chases payment certificates and lobbies for new jobs. Where a post of responsibility has to be created, it usually goes to a close relation, preferably a son. Sometimes this works out well, as trust is repaid with diligence. But equally often the firm turns into a fragile one-man band, which is liable to collapse when it loses the driving force of the original owner. The same problems of suspicion and mutual mistrust inhibit the merger of small firms to create more viable units, which would otherwise be a way of achieving a more balanced spread of domestic construction capacity. A further problem with the many mixed trading and contracting enterprises is that the accounting system is so rudimentary that the proprietor is unable to distinguish the loss-making from the profitable parts of his business. Thus he may regard contracting as profitable simply because he fails to charge a realistic proportion of overheads and financing costs against this activity. Despite this lack of financial measurement, an increasing number of general traders are coming to appreciate that contracting is not so lucrative as it sometimes appears, and there is no profitable half-way house between withdrawal and all-out commitment.

Table 8 summarizes the certifying officer's remarks as at 31 December 1978 on the progress of work on all feeder and trunk road projects, and a total of 149 building projects, in the Greater Accra region—since when the situation has deteriorated rather than improved.

As a result of slow progress, abandonment, termination and suspension many projects in the country are running far behind schedule. Table 9 gives details of original estimated dates of completion of all the 64 on-going trunk road projects and 40 building projects as at the end of 1978.

The figures show that at the time the progress reports were prepared, 69 per cent of all the trunk road projects going on in Ghana and 90 per cent of the 40 building projects considered had failed to meet their target dates of completion. Some had overshot their completion dates by three, four or even five years. These latter tables illustrate the effect of the continuing problems that plague the Ghana construction scene. Next we need to examine the framework of legislation and procedures under which the industry operates, and

Table 8 National feeder- and trunk-road programmes and some building projects in Accra; progress report, 31 December 1978.

Remarks	Feeder roads (No.)	Trunk roads (No.)	Buildings (No.)
Satisfactory progress	170	22	31
Slow progress	82	11	85
Work abandoned due to lack of materials or plant	22	11	—
Work abandoned by contractor	70	14	4
Terminated and re-awarded	10	—	1
Work not started	27	2	5
Work suspended	5	—	—
Contractor concentrating on another job	8	1	—
Work completed	12	3	23
Total	406	64	149

Table 9   Original estimated completion dates for on-going projects, 31 December 1978.

	1973	1974	1975	1976	1977	1978	1979	1980	1981	Completed	Total
Trunk roads	1	4	10	12	7	10	6	9	2	3	64
Buildings	—	5	7	3	15	6	1	1	—	2	40

determine whether they are sufficiently flexible to accommodate the changing needs of a rapidly developing industry and a sharply fluctuating economic environment.

Procedures and Systems

At independence the new Ghana Government inherited a pattern of construction design and execution closely modelled on the traditional British approach, with few concessions to local customs, experience and needs. This approach, although administratively sound, is extremely rigid and compartmentalized, and tends to inhibit innovation in both the technical and management aspects of implementing construction programmes. The compartmentalization is particularly marked for building projects, due to the application of what Bowley[14] describes as the 'system' of a separation of the three phases that lead to the completion of a building:

(i) Working out the overall design in accordance with the client's requirements for accommodation and amenities.
(ii) Calculating the structural design to ensure that the building is durable, resists anticipated loadings and climatic conditions and that the services work.
(iii) Actually producing the building and making it ready for occupation.

In broad terms the first phase is the speciality of the architect, the second of the structural, civil or services engineer, and the third the province of the building contractor who is only involved after the design phases are complete and tender documents prepared. Thus the contractor has no opportunity to apply his experience at the design stage or discuss with the client ways in which his objectives could be achieved more economically. On this watertight division of responsibilities, Bowley comments:[14]

> In sum, the separation of design responsibilities from building responsibility enabled builders to neglect their own education in design, or avoid the employment of designers, and the architect to neglect his own education in building practice and the employment of building technicians. Equally the development of the system of independent quantity surveyors enabled designers to neglect proper study of estimating and avoid the employment of estimators.

Another feature of this 'system' is the absence of competition in design. Although this does have some advantages for the client in that price competitions may be won by incompetent or unscrupulous firms, it does have the effect of insulating the designer from the effects of uneconomic design or inaccurate costings. In fact additional costs accrue to the immediate financial benefit of the consultant because fees are usually calculated as a percentage of overall costs, although it does of course harm his reputation. In the United Kingdom the 'system' of separation of responsibilities has begun to give way in some work areas, particularly the construction of industrial and commercial buildings where there is a trend towards letting 'package deal' design and management contracts. Alternatives are contracts negotiated on a fee basis so that the contractor can be brought in at an earlier stage, and the appointment of project management consultants to co-ordinate all construction management aspects of the job.

In Ghana the traditional system has been preserved more or less intact; indeed a number of additional complications have been introduced. The first step for a would-be construction client is to amass the funds that he will need to pay for his investment. In view of the uncertainties over annual budget votes (let alone forecasting when the funds will actually be available and released) some public sector clients are forced to proceed on a speculative basis, hoping the funds will be made available when needed. Land acquisition is always a difficult and protracted process in Ghana, as the Lands Commission has to approve each application before it is registered at the Deeds Registry in Accra. Since there is no national cadastral survey and survey base maps are obsolete and incomplete, different people may register the same piece of land and land litigation is very common.

Once the client is confident that he has (or will obtain) finance and the title to land on which to build, the next step is to recruit a designer. This is perhaps the easiest stage in the process, since there is a good spread of local consultancy firms capable of coping with all but the most sophisticated and specialist structures. The physical planning and land use regulations also follow the British pattern, so the design drawings have to be submitted to the secretary of the local statutory planning committee leading (in about three-quarters of cases) to the issue of a development permit. The permit normally has a life of two years, after which permission lapses unless a start has been made or an application for renewal made. Armed with his development permit, the prospective developer next visits the local PWD engineer (or city engineer), who is required to examine all applications to build reinforced concrete structures and buildings taller than one storey. Next the regional or district officer of the Ministry of Health looks at the drainage and sewerage plans, and the estimated cost of the building is assessed by the PWD so as to calculate the rateable value (property taxes are, in the British system, calculated as a proportion of the theoretical rent a property might command, even if it is owner-occupied). Only now is the exhausted developer entitled to an actual building permit. Experienced (and wily) clients and their consultants frequently by-pass many of these stages, and there appears to be an informal understanding that public sector clients may be assumed to have complied with government requirements. After the building permit has been obtained the quantity surveyor prepares a bill of quantities upon which bids will be based, and bids are sought from contractors qualified to execute the work. Although bills of quantities are generally prepared for projects valued in excess of 500,000 cedis, smaller jobs are often bid for on the basis of a simple lump sum or schedule of rates.

Although it is broad government policy that all construction work in the public sector should be subject to an open tender procedure, clients can speed up the process by selective tendering or negotiation if they obtain a 'certificate of urgency.' Since there is usually a rush to complete the work once a go ahead has been given, more and more projects have qualified under the certificate of urgency procedure in recent years, so that there is now a discernable trend towards selective tendering or negotiation on the basis of a lump sum price or a schedule of rates. Although the trend away from open tendering on the basis of a bill of quantities suggests an increased risk of malpractice, there are also advantages. Apart from speeding up the project preparation process, the client may well be better served with a few serious, simply-prepared bids from competent contractors than a plethora of 'guesstimates' from incompetent amateurs. Bid preparation is also a costly item for the contractor, particularly for the many small firms who simply cannot cope with the complexities of a bill of quantities and have to hire outsiders to help them.

The evaluation of tenders for large projects (building works valued at over 300,000 cedis and all trunk roads) is done by the Central Tender Board in the Ministry of Finance, on which the Ministry of Works and Housing (or its subsidiaries) are represented. The general procedure is to set a 'target band' of plus or minus ten per cent of the quantity surveyor's estimate (on the grounds that lower bids are frivolous and the contractor would not be able to complete), and award the contract to the lowest satisfactory bid within the 'target band.'

Once the contract has been awarded, the contractor can get to work. On all substantial sites the consultant will be represented on the site by a full-time clerk of works, who is required to check that the required quality standards are maintained and is empowered to issue variation orders and site instructions on the architect's or engineer's behalf. The role of the client's representative is somewhat delicate, since he is paid directly by the client, but the conditions of contract require that he should interpret it in a professional and disinterested fashion, and in effect arbitrate if there is a dispute. When a building is complete, the local building inspector visits the completed premises and must issue a certificate of satisfactory completion before they can be occupied. The contractor remains responsible for faults (other than normal wear and tear) that may develop during the following 'defects liability period' (usually 6 months) and a portion of the contract sum (usually 5 per cent) is retained by the client during this period and only released when all faults have been corrected.

After final acceptance of the structure from the contractor at the conclusion of the defects liability period, maintenance becomes the responsibility of the client organization. Some of the parastatals and the larger private organizations employ maintenance teams working to schedules of preventive maintenance, but the general standards of maintenance are extremely poor, with the result that comparatively new structures deteriorate rapidly and cease to give satisfactory service to their occupants or users.

A Restricting Environment

One of the features of the traditional British system is that the contractor is treated as a lackey rather than as a partner in the construction process, and it is only the last few decades that British contractors have gained emancipation from this subordinate position and begun to bring their expertise to bear in the construction process. Ghanaian contractors have been less fortunate, and there is evidence that unmodified imported institutional framework has been a key factor in holding them back. There are three official sets of articles of agreement and conditions of contract for construction works in Ghana; two for building (with and without quantities) and one for roads and civil engineering. These were based on the forms of contract issued by the Royal Institute of British Architects and the Institution of Civil Engineers, with only minor modifications to suit local conditions. Since the documents have scarcely been modified since they were originally prepared in the pre-independence period, they have not benefitted even from the more recent updating of the British versions and are based on a socio-economic environment that simply does not exist in Ghana. For this reason many of the clauses are merely academic and impossible to implement. A particular problem is the wide powers granted to the architect or engineer under the British System, which is seen as safeguarding the client's interest without adequate regard to the needs of the contractor. Indeed few of the smaller contractors even understand the rather complicated legal wording of the documents, and fewer still would be in a position to avail themselves of their formal rights (for example, terminating the contract if the client defaults on payments), while obligations favourable to the client are rigorously enforced.

A further problem for contractors is the inadequacy of most contract drawings, which contain numerous discrepancies that are left to be sorted out on the site. Bills of quantities are also not always reliable, so that cautious contractors need to check back against the drawings when preparing their estimates. Specifications too give rise to trouble, since standard materials and workmanship specifications are extremely conservative in the light of current shortages. In the One Year Development Plan 1970–1 the government noted:[15]

In many instances construction standards have been set too high for the requirements . . . and costs have therefore been higher than they could have been.

Local standards and codes of practice, appropriate to Ghana's climate, socio-economic and physical environment, have yet to be developed. Indeed one still sees specifications referring to British Standard Specifications (BSS) or Codes of Practice (CP) when describing acceptable standards of workmanship. The current Ghanaian specifications lay down in great detail the type of materials to be used and, at least by implication, how the job is to be done. It may be that a move to a more flexible form of performance specification would be more appropriate for conditions in a country such as Ghana, so that more discretion on materials and methods is left to the contractor providing the final structure is deemed satisfactory. It should be noted that the British system of very circumscribed regulation of materials and methodology only works if interpreted reasonably by an experienced clerk of works on the site. It is generally accepted that a vindictive clerk of works could usually turn it into a weapon to bankrupt a contractor who did not know his rights under the contract. Thus the British system depends implicitly on good communications between well-balanced clients' representatives and contractors, with both parties able and willing to interpret the contract conditions liberally when they are over-rigid, while sticking closely to those with a crucial structural significance. This steady state situation simply does not obtain in Ghana. Inexperienced clerks of works stand rigidly by 'the letter rather than the spirit of the law' in specifications, because they have not acquired sufficient judgement to know when the requirements can be safely relaxed. Meanwhile contractors are unaware of their countervailing rights under the contract, and so boost their bid prices as the only form of protection available to them. No-one gains from inappropriate specifications and their attendant, if unquantified, costs. In the long run the bill for unnecessarily high standards is paid unknowingly by the clients, mostly in the desperately impoverished public sector.

A further factor upon which the current system implicitly depends is good communications. Problems identified on the site can easily be sorted out in the United Kingdom where a quick telephone call to the consultant's head office results in an amended drawing reaching the clerk of works by return of post. In Ghana the postal and telecommunications services do not permit this kind of smooth and expeditious correspondence between the parties, with the result that minor problems can give rise to long delays. Poor communications can also lead to contractors receiving directions directly from the client or his unaccredited representative (e.g. the headmaster of a school under construction). This should never occur under the British system, where all instructions should be directed through the architect or engineer, and the contractor is faced with the dilemma of either upsetting his client or risking not being paid for the additional work.

The Lessons

The performance of Ghana's construction industry has been closely related to that of the economy as a whole, although its ups and downs have usually amplified those in the general economy. Unfortunately there have been more downs than ups in recent years, and the economy has not shown any consistent growth since the boom years of the early 1960s. Bearing in mind the high population growth rate of 2·7 per cent, real standards of living have not increased since independence. Since 1975, the country's economic problems have worsened still further with severe balance of payments and budgetary deficits, escalating inflation, high unemployment and shortages of both consumer and capital goods. In addition, the existing public assets and infrastructure have deteriorated considerably. This has not formed a promising backcloth for construction industry development and, sure enough, its participants have suffered along with the rest.

The framework, the organization and the process of construction in Ghana continue to mirror that in Britain to an almost uncanny degree, with few concessions to the very different national objectives, physical and socio-economic operating environment and construction industry development needs that obtain in Ghana. Professional responsibilities continue to be highly compartmentalized so that inadequate performance by any one of them delays and confuses the whole project, and the contractor occupies a distinctly subordinate position in which he can neither bring his practical experience to bear until after the project design is fixed nor obtain a clear view of his role in the overall construction process. No attempt has been made to modify contract law, contract documents and standard specifications to suit local conditions, so the scope for developing more appropriate kinds of technology and operational procedures is artificially restricted. Domestic contractors find themselves at a severe competitive disadvantage since they find the documents and bills of quantities hard to understand and irrelevant to their circumstances. Their irrelevance is indicated by the frequency with which the various participants (knowingly or unknowingly) contravene contract provisions, the client supplying inadequate information and paying late while the contractor fails to maintain quality standards and overruns the contract period. In fact few contractors are aware of their obligations under the contract, and fewer still are in a position to avail themselves of their rights.

If it is accepted that the problem of a transferred and in many ways inappropriate framework is the root of many of the ills affecting Ghana's construction industry, we should also note that this root has been nourished by the unco-ordinated and frequently-changing bureaucracy that oversees it. The construction industry is, like an ocean liner, slow to change course. This essential inertia of the industry is unfortunately rarely appreciated by non-technical politicians and administrators, and Ghana is no exception to the general rule. Thus there has been a history of sudden changes in public investment programmes made in the hope of an instant response. The changing pattern of public administration has also bred confusion and incoherence, and the Ministry of Works and Housing (itself the subject of frequent internal reorganization) has lacked the prestige and resources that would be needed to give a firm lead.

Will Ghana regain the lost initiative? It is perhaps too early to say. The resources remain; a hard-working people, useful mineral resources and a strong agricultural potential. It is fair to say that whilst the economic vicissitudes have actively worked against the development of the indigenous construction sector, the institutional constraints also play an active role in inhibiting its growth.

CHAPTER 4
The Case of Sri Lanka*

The Environment

Sri Lanka is the eighteenth poorest country in the world, its GNP per capita, less than half that of Ghana, putting it in the bottom half of the World Bank's table of low-income countries. Share its GNP among its 15 million people, and you get an average of only $220 a year. Yet, in the words of a recent *Economist* survey:[1]

> It is quite unlike any other country with that sort of income, and in ways which make it easy for the casual observer to misjudge Sri Lanka's poverty (or which make GNP seem a nonsensical measure of anything except GNP).

Indeed the social statistics tell a happier story, more in line with the gentle beauty of the island itself. Life expectancy at birth is 69 years, only 4 years less than that for the United States. Adult literacy is about 80 per cent, more than twice the figure for Ghana, and an even larger proportion of Sri Lankan children are today enrolled in primary school. The battle against malnutrition has also been fought with impressive success, and in 1977 the average Sri Lankan consumed more than 95 per cent of the calories needed for good health. So the *Economist* survey appears justified in describing Sri Lanka as 'a poor country that has somehow avoided the harshness of its neighbours' poverty.'

What of the construction industry? As in Ghana, the transferred British 'system' retains a powerful influence, with a strict separation of design and supervision responsibilities from building responsibility, and contractual procedures that have been only marginally modified to suit local needs. Political influences have also been marked, with dramatic shifts in policies regarding institutional

---

* This chapter is based on the work of S. Ganesan and in particular: S. Ganesan, 'The construction industry in Sri Lanka', mimeographed *World Employment Programme Working Paper*, restricted (Geneva, ILO, 1982).

arrangements, financing systems, design and construction technology. Thus, as in the Ghana case, we have the opportunity to study the behaviour of the somewhat inflexible (but well-proven in its home environment) British institutional framework when faced with stresses resulting from policy and demand fluctuations that are much more intensive than it was designed to bear.

Sri Lanka has benefitted from a more gradual and sustained social development than many third world countries. In 1900 the island's literacy rate was already higher than Pakistan's and Bangladesh's are today. This stability perhaps also owes something to the predominant Buddhist faith. In any event, it has shown itself in an acceptance of the will of the majority expressed through the ballot box.

The policies pursued by successive governments have varied. For the first 30 years after independence, economic policies were protectionist and paternalistic, with modest growth in construction demand reflecting a respectable—but not startling—growth in GNP per capita of 2 per cent over the period 1960-78. The centralist tendency became more noticeable in 1970 with the election of a new Sri Lanka Freedom Party government which placed its faith in public sector construction capability (although the local contracting sector had by then reached a stage where it was able to cope reasonably comfortably with the demands for its services). As the new policy was implemented private contractors were forced to run down their plant and managerial resources, while a number of new state direct labour organizations sprang up to take their place. An example of this was the Territorial Civil Engineering Organisation (TCEO), which was formed by amalgamating resources from specialized departments such as irrigation, highways and water supply to maximize the use of scarce construction resources in the districts. The then Ministry of Irrigation, Power and Highways gave the rationale for its formation as 'the continuance of departmental institutions and functions that existed earlier was not conducive to the speedy execution of development works'.

In 1977, the new government set about a radical transformation of the island's economy, with significant implications for the construction industry. In the wave of change the TCEO was a minor casualty and disbanded with the comment that 'it has not worked well . . . the organisation cut across the principles of specialization which are basic to modern development'. Both arguments are tenable, but the creation and dissolution of the TCEO must have led to a serious disruption of ongoing work programmes and diverted the efforts of hard-pressed professionals from their main task.

The political stance of the new government in 1977 was quite unlike those of successive governments in the previous 30 years of independence. Import and price controls were scrapped, taxes were lowered, the currency was devalued by 46 per cent, an ambitious new development plan was drawn up and foreign loans were sought to finance it. In the words of the *Economist* survey cited earlier, the new Government's economic model was Singapore while previous governments saw the island as a kind of offshore Burma. The strategy was to tip the scales in favour of the producers, in the belief that consumers would ultimately benefit as well.

The construction industry was affected in two fundamental ways: a massive prospective increase in demand coupled with a new emphasis on execution through the private sector. The increase in demand was powered by three major capital projects; an irrigation and hydro-electric scheme based on dams in the centre of the island, a new capital city four miles east of Colombo and a programme to build 100,000 new houses. Much of the design work for the new projects was to be dealt with by private consultants, and the physical construction work was to be mainly put into the hands of private contractors.

The Mahaweli development project had been started in 1970, when it was envisaged as a 30 year plan to be implemented in three separate phases. The aim was to utilize the 6 million acre feet of water in the Mahaweli river, which had the potential to irrigate about 360,000 ha (compared to an as-then irrigated area of 400,000 ha) and provide over 500 MW of power (compared to an installed capacity of 381 MW). Thus there was an ultimate prospect of almost doubling the irrigated area available for agriculture and more than doubling the nation's power output (with the bonus that the addition would be wholly utilizing a renewable energy source). By 1977 work was still progressing on phase I of the master plan, consisting of dams, tunnels and power plant at Bowatana and Polgolla.

In 1977 the new government decided to attempt to complete the remainder of the project in no more than six years. Fortunately the proposal caught the imagination of outside donors: almost immediately aid was promised for about half the programme's total costs (and two thirds of its foreign currency costs). But, the Sri Lanka government initially underestimated the size—and cost—of the task.

The 1978 estimate of Rs 11,000 million ($600 m)* had escalated to Rs 20,000 million by February 1980 and showed every sign of rising still further. Thus the government decided to lower its sights and go for three dams instead of five, which would still irrigate 50,000 ha and yield an impressive 275 MW of power. Even so, the project cost was still going to exceed the original Rs 12,000 million ceiling by about 50 per cent in real terms and account for as much as 29 per cent of all public sector investment over the period 1980–84.

The *Economist* survey notes that:

> On its own, Mahaweli would have given Sri Lanka's construction industry indigestion. For years, the industry had languished: skilled craftsmen and engineers left for the Middle East in droves, there was a lack of demand and, even more, of building materials. Between 1970 and 1977 the industry's output fell 17 per cent. Suddenly, it was asked to undertake the country's largest ever construction project—with help from foreign contractors, of course, but they were allowed to bring in relatively few skilled people.

The second major construction project, the new capital city at Kotte, was to proceed at a more modest pace. Rs 550 million were budgetted over the period 1980–81 to provide a new parliamentary building and two administrative blocks, and earlier plans for a hostel for members of parliament were postponed. A useful secondary objective in setting up the new capital was to encourage a more satisfactory physical development of Colombo, which had hitherto been constrained to a narrow north-south axis. By reclaiming the 600 acres of marshy land at Kotte the Government planned to redirect future expansion to the east, and gradually achieve a more balanced city layout.

The third area of substantially increased construction demand was housing. In 1973 the previous government had identified the housing shortage as a key social problem and initiated a self-help housing programme, but had never effectively followed it through. The new government set up a committee under the Ministry of Local Government, Housing and Construction, which recommended a programme to construct no less than 100,000 houses over a six-year period, half in Colombo and the remainder split equally between provincial towns and rural areas. Although clearly ambitious

---

* (Rs 16 = US$1).

compared to previous performance, and bearing in mind the other demands on the construction industry, the target can also be seen as a modest one unit per annum per 1,000 population. The public sector contribution in Japan, Singapore and Hong Kong ranged from 5–10 units per annum per 1,000 population throughout the 1970's.

Three-quarters of the new houses were to be occupied by people from the low income group and the remainder would go to the lower middle income group. In order to trim the cost of the programme, half of the 100,000 target was to be met by self-help efforts. About 7 per cent of the Government's five-year investment plans had originally been allocated to housing and urban development, but the rapid rise in construction costs has pushed that share up to $12\frac{1}{2}$ per cent. Even so, it seems likely that the 100,000 target will be met, and the costs of $1,000 for self-help houses and $8,000 for contractor-built houses cannot be regarded as excessive.

Testing the capacity of the industry still further, the rapid expansion of public sector demand was accompanied by greater confidence among private sector developers. This was partly due to the general liberalization of the economy, but investment in residential property also became much more attractive with the influx of expatriate personnel and companies. Rents in Colombo are reported to have risen as much as 15-fold since 1977. Another factor in boosting individual house construction was the investment of remittances sent by Sri Lankans working overseas, particularly in the Middle East.

Thus the overall growth in construction demand was beyond the wildest dreams of the run-down private contracting sector at the beginning of 1977. Growth during the three years 1978, 1979 and 1980 was 28 per cent, 21 per cent and 11 per cent respectively, representing an average real annual growth rate as high as 20 per cent. Construction outgrew the national product by almost 3:1 during the period 1978–79, and its contribution to the increasing GNP had reached 15 per cent by 1979.

There was of course a price for this dramatic expansion, and it was paid by the client in the form of increased unit costs. Building materials were an important factor in fuelling this inflation, as the local manufacturers—like the local contractors—had gradually run down their productive resources and there was no time to commission new equipment to cope with demand. Thus contractors, both local and foreign, were forced to import materials and components on an extensive scale, so that the foreign exchange content in most of the major projects reached levels of 50–80 per cent of project costs. The end result, before demand relaxed somewhat and pressures consequently eased, was that the rate of inflation in construction costs peaked at 40–60 per cent per annum on average, and up to 100 per cent per annum on foreign exchange-intensive projects.

Although domestic and foreign private contractors participated to the full in the construction bonanza, the public sector direct labour organizations were left out in the cold. Oddly enough their idle resources, particularly a large pool of skilled workers, were not redeployed. In fact a desperate shortage of skilled construction workers was to prove a second major constraint on output. An additional 30,000 workers were recruited by the industry during 1977–79, but most of these lacked the experience and skills that would have been needed to maintain satisfactory levels of productivity.

Table 10 represents a bold but rough attempt to measure productivity changes over the last decade. It shows a distinct decline over the period 1971–6 while the private contractors were increasingly excluded from the possibility of bidding for new work and the direct labour organizations were recruiting avidly to take their place. Over the remainder of the period there was a sharp recovery, and the productivity index ended the decade just 1 per cent higher. The productivity increase associated with the construction boom was probably due to the increasing proportion of technologically-sophisticated projects, more investment in plant and equipment among local firms and the influx of expatriate contractors with a predilection for capital-intensive production methods.

The Construction Scene

The Ministry of Local Government, Housing and Construction has overall responsibility for the performance of the industry, but there is a good deal of decentralization of decision-making to its departments and to other ministries. One unique feature of the system is the existence of the Sri Lanka Construction Consortium (SLCC); a private organization (formerly the special projects division of the Chamber of Commerce) which assigns work to both contractors and private consultants registered with it. SLCC contracts are executed on a cost plus basis and the main advantage to the client ministry appears to be a more rapid commencement on site, as the contractor

Table 10 Productivity trends in construction

Item	1971	1976	1979
Employment ('000s)	104[1]	120[1]	140[2]
VA (Rs million):			
in current prices	751	1,164	3,218
in constant 1970 prices	708	685	960
VA per worker in current prices	7,200	9,700	21,400
Productivity index (real)	100	84	101

Sources: [1]From *1971, Census Report*, for 1976 despite a drop in VA in constant price terms, there was a noticeable increase in employment through direct labour organizations in the public sector.
[2]*Ministry of Finance and Planning—Public Investment, 1980-4*, reports an increase of 30,000 during 1977-9 (p. 24). Against this, there was outward migration of skilled workers as follows: 1976 (246); 1977 (3,412); 1978 (2,749); 1979 (2,571). Manpower Planning Division, Ministry of Plan Implementation, and reported by Dr. M. E. Joachim.
For other data, *Annual Report* (various years), Central Bank, Sri Lanka.
Note: In all years, seasonal workers whose contribution is marginal/negligible are not included. Therefore, VA per worker is somewhat inflated.

normally starts work on receipt of a letter of intent and tentative estimate from the client department. The contract sum is negotiated with the technical committee of the Ministry of Local Government, Housing and Construction (or client ministry) on the basis of basic cost plus 35 per cent allowance for overheads and profits. The Consortium is remunerated from a 3 per cent service charge deducted from payments to the contractors. Consortium fees to consultants are on a scale ranging from Rs 1,500 for works under Rs 10 million to Rs 15,000 for works in excess of Rs 200 million.

When the SLCC commenced operations in 1977 the review of contractors' capacity was essentially informal, and the Consortium merely undertook to replace contractors whose performance was unsatisfactory. Naturally the prospect of obtaining work at a guaranteed profit margin attracted increasing numbers of both established and would-be contractors, and formal registration procedures for consultants and contractors were introduced in February 1980. By September of that year 369 contracting firms had been accepted onto the SLCC register, classified as follows:

	No.
Capacity	
Less than Rs 750,000	200
Rs 750,000–1·5 million	95
Rs 1·5–5 million	47
greater than Rs 5 million	27
Total	369

The Consortium does not enjoy a monopoly in the award of public sector contracts, and many contractors also register directly with client ministries and obtain most of their work through conventional bidding procedures. However, the SLCC is particularly helpful to smaller firms who are attempting to establish themselves in the market but lack the estimating skills and experience that are necessary to obtain work competitively by conventional bidding procedures.

The comparatively small size of many SLCC projects is illustrated in the following table, which shows the distribution by size and type of projects undertaken by Sri Lankan contractors through the Consortium during 1979:

Table 11 suggests that the overwhelming majority of SLCC projects are buildings (mainly housing), and two-thirds are valued at less than Rs 750,000. What are the prospects for an aspiring local contractor getting a slice of the cake? Reasonably good, according to

Table 11 *Sri Lanka Construction Consortium—distribution of output between firms, 1979.*

Amount of work	Above Rs 5 m.		Rs 5–1·5 m.		Rs 1·5–0·75 m.		Below Rs 0·75 m.	
Type of work	No. of projects	Amount (Rs m.)	No. of projects	Amount (Rs m.)	No. of projects	Amount (Rs m.)	No. of projects	Amount (Rs m.)
Housing (single to two storey)	3	22·2	5	10·1	10	11·5	125	65·4
Housing (multi-storey—three or more storeys)	2	10·5	2	5·8	2	2·6	–	–
Non-residential buildings	6	46·4	9	26·9	20	18·4	48	12·2
Water supply and sewerage projects	–	–	2	3·7	1	1·0	2	0·7
Total	11	79·1	18	46·5	33	32·5	175	78·3

No. of projects = 237
Amount = Rs 236·7 million.

the list of firms on the Consortium's register quoted earlier (the SLCC register figures were for September 1980, so the potential catchment in 1979 was presumably a little smaller). The best prospect of work was enjoyed by the smallest contractors capable of work up to Rs 750,000, where there was almost one job per contractor (although admittedly some contractors probably succeeded in obtaining more than one project). In the other categories there was a still respectable 1 in 3 chance of a contractor finding work through the SLCC.

Comparisons of quality, costs and completion times of SLCC projects versus those let by conventional tender or executed by direct labour organizations are not available but, in principle, this is an interesting and potentially cost-effective way for a government to help develop its domestic contracting industry (providing the firms already possess the requisite technical and management skills, equipment and finance to provide an adequate service). By working through the private sector, it avoids the twin dangers of building up an expensive bureaucracy and stimulating political interference in the sensitive task of project allocation. The great advantage from the government's point of view is that no direct cost has to be met from the public purse, as the SLCC's costs are covered from the levy on the projects it commissions. Against this it must be noted that in some countries unscrupulous contractors have learned to treat cost plus contracts as licences to print money', and rigorous supervision and cost measurement is necessary to ensure a reasonably economical outcome for the client.

In the absence of any form of association of domestic contractors the Consortium has also taken a lead in highlighting their problems and bringing them to the attention of the government. It is of course difficult for the Consortium simultaneously to play the roles of contractors' advocate and intermediary in the contractual process, particularly with limited technical expertise at its disposal, and its unusual status debars it from membership of bodies such as the International Federation of Asian and Western Pacific Contractors. It is therefore in the process of incorporating itself as a non-profit foundation with the unequivocal aim of developing the local construction industry. As such it would become eligible for foreign aid and assistance, and would hope to promote other relevant activities, such as research into local building materials and training of construction workers.

The SLCC has done well to channel close to Rs 2 billion worth of construction work to Sri Lankan contractors during 1977-81, but the need for local firms to become more self-sufficient and form a contractors' association or federation remains. Already the larger and better established contractors are growing restive at their dependence on the Consortium, and prefer to stand on their own feet by competing in open or selective tendering. The SLCC will therefore have to face the subtle conundrum that confronts all contractor support agencies (and business promotion schemes generally): the need to nurture the weak without breaking the risk-taking entrepreneurial spirit of the strong.

Although domestic contractors have responded well to the surge in demand, it was never likely that they could leap to the stage of competing in open competition for large civil engineering works such as the dams and associated works in the accelerated Mahaweli scheme. However one local firm, Ceylon Development Engineers Co. Ltd., has worked on several irrigation and hydro power projects and has achieved pre-qualification with the Department of Highways for roadworks up to Rs 100 million and bridges up to Rs 50 million. In addition three smaller enterprises have achieved registration for substantial road and bridge projects in joint venture with foreign firms.

Nevertheless foreign contractors have been able to take most of the major projects, including the Kotte Parliamentary Complex and the bulk of the accelerated Mahaweli programme. Altogether, overseas contractors were handling Rs 7,000-8,000 million worth of construction projects by late 1980, with an estimated annual output of Rs 2,000-3,000 million.

If private contractors have been struggling to keep up with demand after many years in the doldrums, the public sector direct labour organizations face the less enviable problem of accommodating themselves to a secondary role after their heyday in the early 1970's. Leaving aside the large maintenance forces in the Railway Department, the Port Commission and the Department of Highways, there are three substantial direct labour organizations concerned with new construction:

State Engineering Corporation (SEC)
State Development and Construction Corporation (SDCC)
River Valley Development Board (RVDB)

The SEC was set up in 1962 to help implement major projects in the industrialization programme of the 1960's, since there was no local contracting capacity in this area at the time and the then government preferred a public sector solution to the development of private firms. It grew explosively:[2]

Year	Output (Rs million)	Employment
1963/64	4.8	1,963
1968/69	88·0	10,226
1969/70	84·0	14,072

It was, however, growth at a price, for by 1969/70 it had accumulated losses of Rs 20 million on an invested capital of Rs 33 million, and the Government was sufficiently concerned to set up a special committee to review its performance.[2] Although the financial performance left much to be desired, there were positive aspects. The massive Tulhiriya factory complex worth Rs 200 million had been completed within two years, and the Review Committee noted that 'it gave an opportunity to "Ceylonese engineers" to gain valuable experience through direct involvement in the construction and supervision of large civil engineering works, on a scale unavailable in this country at any previous date.' The main cause of the poor financial results was found to be an excessive build up of plant and labour to execute the works; by 1970 the SEC's plant and stock was assessed at between Rs 46 and 50 million for a turnover of around Rs 80 million, while the wage bill itself ran close to Rs 40 million.

By March 1971 accumulated losses had reached Rs 30 million, but the SEC started to run down its excessive work force and also benefitted from the 1970-7 Government's ideological opposition to private contractors by picking up a dominant share of the building work available, particularly multi-storey projects. By 1975 the work force had been trimmed to 12,167 and the financial position looked much healthier. Invested capital had been boosted to Rs 70 million, and income of Rs 118·7 million actually exceeded expenditure (by the margin of Rs 2·4 million). Similar surpluses were achieved in the following two years, while employment declined to 11,049 and 8,862 respectively.

1977 saw the advent of the new government and the SEC, like other direct labour organizations, fell from favour. Employment fell still further to 6,904 in 1978 only, oddly enough, to rise to 7,936 in 1979 and 9,591 in 1980. Output, after adjusting for inflation, appears to have declined steadily. This may partially reflect a switch to projects where labour-intensive techniques are more appropriate (which would also explain the recent upward trend in employment), since almost two-thirds of its work is now in low rise housing. The SEC appears to be reconciled to the passing of the heady pioneering days of the 1960s, and is seeking to survive on the basis of acceptable performance on projects which are less spectacular but nonetheless useful.

The State Development and Construction Corporation (SDCC) derived from the PWD Bridges Organization in 1971 as a major state contractor specializing in bridges, highways, tunnels and other heavy civil engineering works. Trends in output and employment are indicated in Table 12.

After the depressing series of losses, the profit of Rs 20·6 million achieved in 1979 is encouraging. However, the cash flow situation

Table 12 State Development and Construction Corporation—output, employment etc.

Item	1971 (1 Oct. to 31 Dec.	1973	1975	1977	1978	1979
Output (Rs m.)	5·7	18·5	36·5	37·8	51·2	93·5
Employment	–	–	–	–	2,863	4,209
—skilled	–	–	–	–	1,863	1,923
—unskilled	–	–	–	–	1,000	2,286
Expenditure on plant and equipment (Rs m.)	0·012	3·2	2·7	0·6	0·4	3·2
Grant from treasury (Rs m.)	–	–	1·1	18·1	6·0	10·5
Profit (or loss) (Rs m.)	0·9	(1·9)	(2·7)	(0·8)	(2·3)	20·6

– Indicates not available.
Source: SDCC.

remained precarious, with no less than Rs 40 million owing from government clients. It is a world-wide phenomenon in developing countries that, when finance is short, public sector contractors are the last to be paid. The effect is that the managers concerned are forced to devote excessive time to debt collection, and working capital is squeezed to the point that purchases have to be delayed to the last minute, thereby delaying site activities and ultimately resulting in declining performance. The irony is that the outcome is frequently a condemnation of the unfortunate contractor by the very same officials in the treasury and client ministries whose default has led to its downfall.

The River Valleys Development Board (RVDB) was instituted when the government decided to embark on the Uda Walawe (river basin) Development Scheme in the early 1960s. It recruited avidly, and by 1970 more than 8,000 people were at work on the Walawe project. During 1970–3 the government transferred a further 5,000 employees from Gal Oya (RVDB's predecessor) to Walawe in stages, so that by 1972 the total labour strength was up to 13,483.

The problem was that there were now far too many employees for the work available, and it was time to put the whole recruitment exercise into reverse. A voluntary redundancy programme in 1973 was followed by a costly retrenchment exercise in 1976, resulting in nearly 4,500 employees losing their jobs.

The RVDB then launched itself ambitiously into contract work (having first experimented with this activity in 1974). The results were disastrous, with accumulated losses during 1974–8 amounting to over Rs 23 million which stimulated another government review committee.[3] If the findings of the earlier review committee into the financial performance of the SEC were disquieting, the figures unearthed by the RVDB committee were staggering, with contract losses in 1977 almost reaching 100 per cent of turnover (see Table 13.)

Since the RVDB used predominantly labour-intensive technologies, it is not surprising that labour recruitment and management were found to be at the root of its troubles. The committee found that the limited RVDB management were simply unable to cope with an excessive labour force with a serious imbalance of skills, exacerbated by the 'refusal of the permanent employees to do manual work, at least the majority of them'. However, another contributory factor has been the reluctance of the RVDB's clients to adequately fund its activities. In 1979, an average of 5,521 employees (just over half the total workforce) were still engaged on the multi-purpose development of the Walawe river valley, and their wage and salary bill alone was Rs 36 million. This was to be financed by government grant; yet in fact only Rs 33 million was made available for the scheme as a whole, of which Rs 18·5 million was available for capital works. Since the funds were not even sufficient to meet the labour wages, work ground to a virtual standstill. The remaining 4,500 or so employees were engaged on contract work for clients such as the Mahaweli Development Board.

Turning to design and supervision, prior to 1977 there were only a handful of private consultants and the lion's share was in the hands of the engineers and other professionals attached to various government agencies (supplemented by foreign consultants for occasional specialist work). As the SLCC began to allocate design work to private firms, significant numbers of engineers, architects and others started to see a future in private practice. By 1979, 43 firms had registered with the Consortium and were sharing in the 503 projects (worth in total more than Rs 400 million) allocated during that year.

Government departments continue to be involved in a good deal of civil and structural design, and there are also two significant parastatals in this sector. The SEC consultancy division has steadily increased its turnover to around Rs 30 million, and the Central Engineering Consultancy Bureau (which is rather larger) enjoys a particularly good professional reputation and has made a major contribution to the design and implementation of the accelerated Mahaweli programme.

Sri Lanka has long been a net exporter of engineering talent, and this has become an increasingly serious drain on the pool of

Table 13   Performance of River Valley Devt. Board contract jobs

Year	Value of work (Rs m.)	Profit or (loss) (Rs m.)
1976	10·5	(5·2)
1977	14·9	(14·5)[1]
1978	58·1	(4·7)
1979 (Jan–June)	29·3	(2·4)

[1] This extraordinarily large loss compared with turnover arose mainly from a single project (Dambula Oya Reservoir) where the loss was 90% of contract value.

professional engineering skills since the early 1970s. Fortunately the pool of qualified engineers (currently between 2,500 and 3,000) is itself much larger than in many developing countries, and it is supplemented each year with 300 new graduates. Even so the continuing loss of skills is a serious matter when the industry is under such intense pressure, and from 1977 to 1979 a further 140 engineers (and close to 9,000 skilled construction personnel) went to Middle East countries alone. On a brighter note, most retain their roots in the island and many are likely to return with enhanced skills (and a little capital) to contribute more effectively to the industry's performance in future years.

Procedures and Systems

The construction framework in Sri Lanka is, like that in Ghana, founded on the received 'system' of strict separation of responsibility for design from responsibility for construction. Although the general shape of the framework is familiar, it has certain innovative features (like the existence of the Sri Lanka Construction Consortium) and there is also an unusual degree of latitude granted to individual departments in their standards and contractual procedures.

The framework will therefore be examined stage by stage under five headings:

(i) Registration of Contractors.
(ii) Types of Contract.
(iii) Contract Awards.
(iv) Specifications.
(v) Conditions of contract.

Registration of contractors

There is no central system of contractor registration in Sri Lanka, and most major client departments maintain their own registers based on the usual criteria of financial worth, plant inventory, previous experience and availability of qualified staff (although giving different weightings to the various factors). As stated earlier, the SLCC has its own system of registration which is essentially geared to the encouragement of smaller firms (and backed up by an offer to replace contractors who perform badly). Client departments with their own registration procedures are naturally more interested in getting their projects built without bother by securing competent contractors (and safeguarding their position in the event of default).

Thus the Department of Highways requires evidence of satisfactory completion of previous jobs, but also a report from the Divisional Revenue Officer/Assistant Government Agent on the 'financial worth and general standing of the applicant.' In addition, for jobs worth over Rs 1 million a competent civil engineer should be employed.

The Department of Buildings also requires applicants for larger jobs to employ a qualified engineer, and provide evidence of previous experience. The financial worth provision is, however, relatively harsh and the contractor or his firm must show fixed assets to the value of 25 per cent of the registration sought. For example, a Group A contractor hoping to work on projects in excess of Rs 1·5 million should show assets of Rs 0·4 million. Even with the recent escalation in property values this can be a difficult hurdle and, to add insult to injury, the unfortunate applicant has to pay 1 per cent of the certificate of worth to the Assistant Government Agent or Divisional Revenue Officer for having established the value of assets.

The Irrigation Department has its own special rules for small and medium size contractors. In the case of small contractors a certificate of worth in excess of Rs 15,000 must be obtained from the *Gramasevaka* (who replaced the village headman), together with a written confirmation that the applicant has been a subcontractor on similar work. He can then bid for individual contracts up to three times his net worth, and can take on work to an aggregate value of six times his certificate of worth. Contractors for medium-size jobs (Rs 15,000–100,000) can be assessed on the basis of either net worth or four times annual income. The Department places less stress on experience, providing the applicant has a satisfactory certificate of worth, together with adequate plant and skilled staff.

The National Water Supply and Drainage Board uses a pre-qualification procedure for major projects rather than maintaining a formal register. Since this is a specialised field most potential contractors are well known to the Board.

Overseas contractors are registered centrally by the Ministry of Local Government, Housing and Construction.

Types of contract
Sri Lanka inherited the system of open tendering based upon bills of quantities, and this persisted for the first three decades after

independence with only minor variations. The rush of new work in 1977 proved a major test for this rather rigid and time-consuming system, and it began to break down under the pressure of events. Several departments tried to limit the workload by resorting to selective tendering, but even this requires careful attention to pre-qualification, and the need to prepare detailed drawings and contract documents is of course unaltered. Under pressure to get contracts moving, several departments took the further step of resorting to negotiated contracts as a rule rather than an exception. It remains to be seen whether the auditors' reports on these jobs will eventually vindicate this move.

Several clients have experimented with alternatives to the standard measured contract based on a bill of quantities which is still the firm favourite in the Department of Buildings and the National Water Supply and Drainage Board. Examples are 'lump sum' contracts (sometimes modified to allow for limited materials price increases), 'cost plus fixed fee', 'target price' (in which the contractor shares in savings or excess in relation to an agreed initial estimate) and 'cost plus percentage fee' (favoured by the SDCC and the SEC).

Contract awards

Methods of awarding contracts again vary considerably from department to department. The Department of Buildings generally accepts bids from contractors within a specific capacity group (i.e. deters 'plundering' by Group A contractors seeking to bid for projects in Groups B or C), although it has made increased use of negotiation through the SLCC since 1977. The Ministry of Education has similar procedures but with the difference that, where possible, it channels work through the School Development Societies (which limit themselves to a 10 per cent profit margin). The Department of Irrigation permits its Regional Irrigation Engineers to commission tenders up to Rs 100,000, and some tasks are executed by Rural Development Societies or Cultivation Committees on a negotiated basis.

The Mahaweli Development Board prefers selective tendering (usually from a group of about 10 pre-qualified firms), but sometimes negotiates standard jobs on the basis of an agreed schedule of rates set by the parent ministry. The Water Supply and Drainage Board, however, generally uses open tendering, but sometimes resorts to selective tendering (although only occasionally to negotiation). Both it and the Port Commission sometimes have to invite bids from foreign contractors for specialist work, such as sewer-lining or dredging, although suitable local firms are free to bid.

The Urban Development Authority has channelled a useful number of its smaller jobs to local firms through the SLCC, but 90 per cent by value of its larger specialist projects have gone to foreign contractors.

The SEC and SDCC still retain some privileges as construction parastatals in that they are exempted from some of the pre-qualification requirements (e.g. minimum plant holdings, financial assets, etc.) and are able to negotiate lump sum contracts on the basis of agreed rates with organisations such as the Mahaweli Development Board, the Fisheries Corporation and the Irrigation Department. These jobs can be quite substantial; the SDCC has negotiated a road and bridge project with the Mahaweli Board worth as much as Rs 120 million.

Specifications

Specifications are perhaps the least glamorous of the links that make up the construction framework, and consequently the least frequently reviewed and revised. This is a pity, since their influence on the shape and performance of the industry is as powerful as it is subtle. Ideally, in a developing country, specifications should define and promote appropriate technological choices arising from diversified demand. In this task they should emphasize the use of indigenous resources and local building skills, and avoid the temptation to 'play it safe' by over-specification. If these criteria are not satisfied specifications can be wasteful, can lead to an inappropriate technology and can retard construction development.

The general specifications for building and housing currently in use in Sri Lanka remain the *Standard Specification: Building* of the 'Public Works Department, Ceylon' revised in 1961, but still bearing the marks of the original edition prepared prior to independence in 1946. These specifications had been worked out from the then current British Standards, with some modifications to suit conditions on the island at the time. There has often been talk of revisions to accommodate more suitable materials and methods, but there has somehow never been time to get down to it. To be fair, the work involved in the task of revision should not be minimized; incorporation of local materials implies a substantial programme of testing, establishment of new standards and devising new methods for quality control.

An example of the foregone potential for savings through the introduction of appropriate specifications is in low income housing; one of the priority areas for recent government investment and one in which foreign materials and foreign contractors have been allowed to gain a surprisingly strong foothold. The specifications and the designs which arise from them combine to discourage the use of local materials. For example, heavy reinforced concrete frames have been preferred to load bearing bricks even in two storey dwellings, due to indifferent quality control and lack of standards for local brick manufacture. Other examples are the use of cement-based plaster instead of lime-sand mortar, and reinforced concrete pads instead of rubble foundations.

Indeed the whole design philosophy can be questioned. When needs are so pressing and resources so short, would it not be sensible to emulate the post-war Japanese policy of promoting shorter life houses? This option does not seem to have been discussed, let alone explored.

The most common fault in Sri Lanka specifications is over-caution, probably stemming from earlier suspicions regarding the technical competence of local contractors, so that the factor of safety was expanded to include a 'factor of ignorance.' Unfortunately the costs of over-specification rarely come to light. However, one example of the difficulties that can arise was the aggregate specifications on the Bowatenne project undertaken by the SDCC, which were so tight that special crushers were required. Another example was an official circular asking contractors to use bricks produced to Sri Lankan standards when it was known that hardly any such bricks were currently being produced by the local industry!

The end result of over-specification tends to be under-enforcement, since practical clerks-of-works recognize that contractors cannot achieve the impossible. This is, however, an unsatisfactory way of compensating for over-rigid standards, since less-experienced inspectors may relax other standards where factors of safety are less generous, thereby endangering the finished structure.

Conditions of contract
There are no general conditions of contract in Sri Lanka, although the Attorney General's Department is consulted on the conditions set

by individual public sector agencies, and overseas-financed work is normally subject to the conditions laid down by the Fédération Internationale des Ingénieurs Conseils (FIDIC).

Only the Irrigation Department reserves the lower categories of its projects for domestic contractors, and these contractors frequently complain that there is an implicit bias against them in the requirements laid down by the various public sector client agencies regarding financial status, bonding, penalty clauses, guarantees and limits to price escalation payments. Some of these aspects are reviewed in the following paragraphs.

Liquidated damages: The general level of liquidated damages is 1/4000 of the value of the contract for each day of delay beyond the contract period (plus any authorized extension), although the People's Bank (more pessimistically) operates an alternative of $\frac{1}{2}$ per cent of contract value per month of delay. In fact, as in the United Kingdom, the courts are reluctant to accept any punitive element and require liquidated damages to be limited to 'a reasonable pre-estimate of actual damage which will or may be sustained by the client on reason of the aforesaid default of the contractor.' Thus the apparently frightening liquidated damages clause is something of a paper tiger, and the Department of Buildings is reported to have hardly imposed any damages during the period 1978–9. Nevertheless the risk of having to pay substantial liquidated damages adds to the uncertainties of a contractor's operations, and gives rise to a contingency item in his balance sheet that may well deter potential lenders if he seeks external capital.

Bonds and Retention: Whilst the layman may think it is the contractor who builds and the client who pays, the practice is not quite so simple. First the would-be contractor has to pay a (fairly small) non-refundable fee to get hold of the contract documents. Then he must provide a bid bond to show good faith when he puts in his tender. If he is awarded the job, a performance bond will be required. Then, just to be on the safe side, the client will keep back a percentage 'retention' from all his payments. Naturally the contractor will inflate his bid to cover the costs of these items. But it is the small local contractor with limited finances who finds bonds and borrowing expensive, while multinational firms have ready access to extensive banking facilities and can make such arrangements as a matter of routine.

Bid bonds are normally limited to the larger jobs, but they can be onerous for local firms seeking to wrest work from foreign companies. For example, a contractor wishing to bid for the Victoria Dam project (worth about Rs 1·5 billion) had to find either a cash deposit of Rs 10 million or obtain an equivalent bond from an approved bank. The standard performance bond is 2½ per cent of contract value, although it is higher on larger jobs (10 per cent for the Victoria Dam project). Small contractors often experience difficulty in obtaining performance bonds, since banks require a cash deposit of up to 75 per cent of bond value to offset their risks. Bid bonds are not called for on SLCC contracts, although a 2½ per cent performance bond is necessary and a 5 per cent retention deduction is made from certified payments. The state contractors (SDCC and SEC) are in the advantageous position of having all bonding requirements waived on their contracts.

Advances and Financial Guarantees: Contractors working for the Ministry of Local Government, Housing and Construction are relatively fortunate (compared to their brethren in other developing countries) in being able to secure mobilization advances of 20 per cent, subject to the provision of a bank guarantee. The Irrigation Department, however, only offers this facility to contractors working through the SLCC.

Local contractors have appealed for an increase to 35 per cent on civil engineering contracts, to take account of payment delays and the need to stockpile materials. A more serious complaint is the difficulty of obtaining guarantees (which, like bonds, are much more difficult for local firms to secure), and it has been suggested that guarantees should be waived for pre-qualified domestic contractors with a good track record.

Price Escalation: Inflation in wage and materials costs has become more acute during the recent boom, and non- or under-recovery of costs is a serious matter for the contractor. The causes are several. Firstly, some clients exclude certain materials from price escalation clauses (many irrigation contracts limit price adjustments to cement, steel and petroleum products). Secondly, materials price recovery is limited to official prices, while it may be impossible to procure key materials other than on the black market. Similarly wage escalation is based on Wages Board scales, while the supply-demand position may allow skilled workers to command premium rates. Finally, delays in cost recovery of up to $2\frac{1}{2}$ months are not uncommon. In response to these problems and the cash flow difficulties that they cause, contractors are calling for automatic reimbursement of price increases according to agreed indices of materials and labour costs.

The broad picture is of a framework which remains alien and which has, despite various additions and amendments to meet specific complaints and anomalies, never been subjected to root and branch review. Its main weakness is that it offers little comfort or encouragement to the growth and development of local materials, local skills and the local industry. For example, no attempt has been made to 'slice and package' projects so that they are of a size with which local firms can cope. The scope for this on the various housing and general building schemes which have fallen recently to contractors from France, India, Italy, Japan, the Republic of Korea, Singapore and the United Kingdom would appear to be definitely neglected. Foreign-financed projects seem particularly difficult for domestic contractors to penetrate, although it is their experience that they have a better chance on projects under World Bank or Asian Development Bank conditions than on those with bilateral aid financing.

Problems

Apart from the problems stemming from the institutional framework, there are others which relate to the operating environment.

Materials Supplies: It was inevitable that the sudden surge in construction output after a long period in the doldrums should generate materials shortages. Larger contractors react by stockpiling key materials, but most small firms cannot afford to tie up capital in this way. It is also difficult to find local materials that match the rather stiff specifications when supplies are short, so clients are sometimes forced to relax standards in the interests of prompt completion. Obtaining imported materials is expensive for local contractors who have to make substantial advance payments to the shippers, although the Ministry of Local Government, Housing and Construction is considering making advance payments for 'materials on site' on receipt of a certificate confirming the advance payment.

Plant and Equipment: There is a dearth of long-term finance for equipment purchase, which effectively precludes local firms from building up the plant inventories that they need to prequalify for major civil engineering contracts. Banks generally regard construction equipment loans as high risk propositions, and often require a 50 per cent guarantee in addition to the security of the plant itself. However, the National Development Bank has made contractors eligible for loans up to Rs 1 million under its medium and small industries assistance programme, and consideration has been given to a much more ambitious scheme for providing construction plant through a new joint company with a large Japanese leasing specialist. Smaller contractors generally prefer to limit their financial outlay and risk by hiring plant as and when they need it. However, the plant hire market on the island is poorly developed, and rates sometimes appear excessive. In response to this problem, the Irrigation Department sometimes assists its contractors by making available plant from its own extensive inventory at relatively favourable hire rates.

Cash Flow: One of the features of contracting as a commercial activity is the irregularity of cash flow. The theory is simple; expenditure proceeds in a gentle 'S' curve while receipts come in regular steps. Thus, somewhere between half and two-thirds of the way through the job, cumulative income overtakes cumulative expenditure and all is well. The truth is often more harsh. Poor estimating may lead to an inadequate bid, so a surplus may never emerge. Certified payments may be delayed. The extra cost of variation orders or price escalation may only be recovered months after they have been borne by the unfortunate contractor.

There are two possible causes of cash flow crises: an unsatisfactory operating environment or bad management by the contractor. The contractor always blames the former, while the client usually plumps for the latter. The truth normally lies somewhere between the two extremes, as it almost certainly does in Sri Lanka. Payment delays undoubtedly do occur, often as a result of staff shortages in the client department or delayed remittances of block funds by the treasury. But as often as not the cause is indifferent 'hand to mouth' cash management by the contractor.

Paradoxically such a contractor can be caught in a trap arising out of the generous 20 per cent mobilization advance which boosts his initial cash position and can instil a false air of confidence. The trap emerges at the time of the first interim payment. Suppose Rs 100,000 is certified. This is subject to 10 per cent retention, and recovery of the 20 per cent mobilization advance cuts it further to Rs 70,000. If the contractor is working through the SLCC on a letter of intent and the contract figure has not yet been negotiated, only 75 per cent will be made available to him, bringing the figure down to Rs 52,500. Of this the bank retains 10 per cent for the advance guarantee, leaving the contractor Rs 47,250 (less the Consortium fee of 2 to 3 per cent). Thus, at the time of maximum outlay the contractor can end up with less than half the payment he might have anticipated.

Borrowing: As in many developing countries, the first rule of bankers contemplating advances to domestic contractors is 'when in doubt, don't!' Thus the three major private banks, the Hong Kong and Shanghai Banking Corporation, Grindlays Bank Limited and the Chartered Bank, tend to steer clear of domestic contractors and any lending is subject to strict collateral cover.

The Bank of Ceylon provides performance bonds, letters of guarantee and loans or overdrafts to cover both working capital requirements and purchase of construction equipment. The type and level of security demanded depend on the standing of the customer and can be a cash margin (10–20 per cent of the advance), a third party guarantee or specific collateral (mortgage deeds or life assurance). The Bank's caution has been reflected in a favourable lending experience, with few defaulters.

Despite the efforts of the Bank of Ceylon, domestic contractors continue to experience severe liquidity problems which adversely affect their capacity to serve their clients. Suppliers' credit has almost dried up in recent years as merchants have taken advantage of the sellers' market to tighten their trading terms. In fact some of the parastatals, such as the Building Materials Corporation, have gone so far as to demand advance payments for the privilege of supplying materials.

Thus contractors have no alternative but to turn to the banks, where many feel aggrieved at the lack of understanding of their problems and needs, describing the whole banking system on the island as 'archaic'. It is true that few bankers are able to make an informed judgement on the technical capacity of a contractor to undertake a particular project. But communication is a mutual task and, if the transactions between a contractor and his banker degenerate into a 'dialogue of the deaf', both must share the blame.

The essential trouble is that, while the banker is at a loss with the technical aspects, the contractor lacks the elementary financial skills that he would need to present his requirements in the language of banking, including cash flow charts and the like. Bankers can reasonably suggest that it is the lack of management skills—particularly financial skills—on the part of domestic contractors that makes them unattractive borrowers. This argument leads to the identification of a further problem facing domestic contractors: insufficient exposure to appropriate training facilities.

Training: Construction industry training policy has so far focussed mainly on upgrading artisan skills, although the Centre for Housing, Planning and Building has a programme 'to undertake training for on-site construction managers' consisting of 2–3 month courses for 150 or so middle level site managers a year. Unfortunately for the private contractors, most places on these courses have so far been taken up by participants from the public sector.

A highly ambitious $25 million scheme to provide training for over 55,000 construction workers over a 3-year period has been put forward by the World Bank. This would encourage participation by contractors, but mainly by seconding artisans (who are often employed by sub-contractors) and equipment operators. Thus the crucial construction management skills would still be overlooked, despite the need being recognized by the contractors themselves in a recent plea for 'training in financial management for senior construction personnel.'

Technology

With a low per capita GNP (about $220), low construction employment (12 per 1,000 population) and a growing market, Sri Lanka would seem ideally suited for maximum use of labour-based technologies. The opportunity was identified in the early 1970's when the 1972–6 Five Year Plan deplored 'that even in the construction of buildings and irrigation works when labour-intensive techniques were feasible there was no conscious attempt to use them'.[4]

Part of the trouble has been a reluctance to discriminate between labour-intensive methods and plain inefficiency, particularly in forgotten corners of the public sector. About 100,000 people, or half the national construction labour force, are employed in the state construction and maintenance agencies (the Department of Highways alone has about 60,000), and estimates of over-manning in some of them range from 25 per cent up to a staggering 150 per cent. These inefficiencies have given rise to a feeling that labour-based technologies are by nature inefficient which, although erroneous, is hard to dispel. Further constraints have arisen from the pressure to get new projects underway (so that scarce project preparation staff could not be diverted to amending designs, bills of quantities and specifications to suit labour-based methods), together with a shortage of competent supervisory personnel.

Certainly labour-based technologies can work in Sri Lanka. World Bank/IDA-financed irrigation projects, the Asian Development Bank-financed Kirindi Oya Irrigation and Settlement Project and the Gin Ganga Flood Protection Scheme financed by China have all been reasonably successful. The urgency accorded to the main accelerated Mahaweli project has dictated capital-intensive methods, but the following downstream development contracts may be dealt with more flexibly. Thus the Mahaweli Development Board is experimenting with asking contractors for two tenders: one on a machine-intensive basis and an alternative employing labour-intensive techniques, with a view to favouring the latter on jobs where speedy completion is not critical to the overall programme.

The Lessons

What is not at issue is the remarkable resilience of the Sri Lankan construction industry. Since 1977 it has spearheaded the national drive to faster growth almost single-handed. In the words of the *Economist* survey quoted at the start of this chapter:[1]

> Yet the wonder is that the island's builders have managed as well as they have. Their costs may have risen dramatically, but so has the real value of their output—by an average 25 per cent a year since 1977. Not bad, for an industry that was long becalmed and still feels the pull of the Middle East competition for its workers.

Could a better result have been achieved? Could cost inflation have been mitigated? Could better use have been made of public sector construction capacity (either by giving it more work or by dismantling it completely and recycling its resources to the private sector)? Was it really necessary for foreign firms to take such a substantial share of the work available?

All these are fair questions, although the response should take into account the government's legitimate impatience to get its new policy underway. Perhaps it is only now, after the first shock waves of the boom have passed, that reflection and review are possible.

Undoubtedly a better result might have been achieved if more time had been available to build up indigenous construction capacity in advance of demand. On the whole, domestic contractors have responded well to the calls made upon them, but they could have performed better if demand had advanced more steadily and they had possessed a greater degree of relevant construction management expertise to enable them to make optimum use of the resources at their disposal.

Construction management training remains a priority if domestic contractors are to compete on even terms with foreign firms, and it is clear that local building materials and construction companies would invest more confidently in additional capacity if their market was more assured. The government could help by providing work in a form that favours domestic contractors by 'slicing and packaging' larger projects so that contracts are of a more manageable size. A steadier and more reliable workload would also contribute to mitigating cost inflation in the long run, as contractors would be able to use their resources more efficiently and thereby maintain an equivalent level of profit while accepting lower margins.

The public sector contractors have been in limbo since 1977, as official policy appears to have been one of benign neglect. Certainly life has not been easy for managers of these organizations. Work availability has been sporadic and often unmatched to painstakingly-developed specialist skills; for example the SEC, with innovatory skills in factory construction, now finds itself with two-thirds of its turnover in low-/medium-rise housing. Financial problems abound, as inadequate investment, excessive wage costs and slow payment by clients lead to burgeoning contract losses which further deplete working capital.

Would it be kinder to put these organizations out of their misery? Certainly they continue to tie up scarce resources (particularly skilled manpower) that is in desperately short supply elsewhere. Yet the permanent labour forces relish their security of tenure, and would not willingly switch to private contractors despite the offer of higher wages, while many of the agencies have gained a good reputation for high quality work.

If they are not to be disbanded, then a determined attempt should be made to raise their productivity to acceptable levels. This will not be easy; but the skills and experience are there, and a properly structured incentive system might motivate staff at all levels to introduce the disciplines of time- and cost-consciousness that are currently so sadly lacking.

Turning to the question of the increased use of foreign contractors, this was probably inevitable given the urgency accorded to the construction component of capital investment plans in recent years. Somewhat idealistically the International Federation of Asian and West Pacific Contractors Associations has advised that: 'when contractors seek work in another country they should refrain from competing with domestic contractors on jobs that can be executed by the latter. They should confine themselves to large jobs—complex, high technology jobs'. Bearing this advice in mind, it is perhaps not surprising that no local firm was able to pre-qualify for the complex Victoria arch dam project, but it is definitely disappointing that so many foreign firms have scooped up contracts for housing and general building works. It is also disappointing that relatively few local firms have been able to participate in projects executed by foreign companies either as sub-contractors or (preferably) as joint venture partners.

The consummate ease with which foreign materials and foreign contractors have penetrated the island's construction market suggests that the construction framework remains more attuned to their operations than to the development needs of the indigenous industry. As in the case of Ghana, no real attempt has been made to modify contract law, contract documents and standard specifications to suit local conditions. The operating environment also handicaps the domestic industry, which faces constraints in all the key resources of finance, skilled personnel, plant and materials. Some of these constraints affect all firms alike, but others can be circumvented by the foreign company with its ready access to external supplies.

The reader will recall that the other major lesson of the Ghana study was the damaging effect of unpredictable policy and administrative changes. Interestingly enough, this is also a feature of recent construction history in Sri Lanka. Although changes in the pattern of public administration have been less frenetic than in

Ghana, switches in objectives and strategy have been, if anything, more dramatic. The 1970's started with a government with a strong commitment to the public sector, and which consequently contemplated with equanimity the decline and eventual disappearance of private businesses. Then in 1977 came a new government with a diametrically-opposed ideological approach. Not only was private enterprise to be the prime mover in the construction market, but that market was itself to be strained almost to breaking-point in an effort to engineer capital investment-led growth (with a housing boom into the bargain).

Whilst it must be admitted that the industry has coped surprisingly well with these vicissitudes, one might also ponder how much greater might have been its achievements if the tide of events had been consistently favourable.

CHAPTER 5
Releasing the Constraints

The last two chapters have reviewed the recent (post-independence) history of the construction industry in two very different countries in two continents. Apart from roughly equivalent populations, the only common factor appears to be the inheritance of a ready-made construction industry framework designed to meet the needs of expatriate administrators. These administrators came from the United Kingdom and they applied the system they knew, with only minor modifications to suit their perception of local requirements. This perception reflected their predominant interest in the *products* rather than the *process* of construction, and consequently the development of indigenous construction capacity was not among their priorities.

It is no mystery how the British system came to be imposed in Ghana or Sri Lanka (or any of the other countries that experienced British colonial rule). What we ultimately need to know is how the transferred framework should be changed to make it more responsive to development needs.

Overall, it appears that the British system works quite satisfactorily when the power which it regulates is well distributed. However, in the cases of Ghana and Sri Lanka, the institutional framework has been subjected to a very different set of pressures and has not worked effectively. The pressures in these cases have come about through radical administrative and policy changes, coupled with a need to develop rapidly domestic construction capacity. This is by no means an unusual combination in the Third World, so there is a case for the designer to return to the drawing board while there is still time.

The reassessment need not imply the abandonment of the present system. Even if a ready-made and perfected alternative were to be available (which it is not), the political, administrative and economic upheaval that would result would be unacceptable.

What we are seeking is a means of modifying the framework so that it can withstand a greater range of stresses and strains than it was designed to cope with in its home environment. The aim is to rejig it so as to provide the best possible long-term service to its ultimate customers, remembering that the majority of these remain the (predominantly rural) poor in developing countries, whose interest is in securing better, simpler, cheaper structures and the economic and social advantages that arise from participating in their provision.

Although the rural poor are in the majority as ultimate customers, they will generally be unable to supply, or even control, the delivery mechanism. The exception is the provision of simple village structures, such as housing, dispensaries and school classrooms. These technologically simple buildings which take two or three months to put together can take ten times as long to wend their way through the bureaucracy. They are often eventually built by a contractor (or direct labour force) from a remote town using external materials and manpower, and 'supervised' by an occasional visit from a young graduate in a Land-Rover. There must be a better way.

The answer, strangely enough, probably lies closer to the original British system than to its now universally accepted replacement. It will be recalled that this system of local commissioning and provision of simple buildings through autonomous 'master masons' controlling local craft teams grew up when resources in the United Kingdom were dispersed, the technology of building was relatively uncomplicated and speed of completion on the site was not a great priority. These conditions are, of course, precisely those which pertain in the rural areas of most developing countries today.

Although the introduction of more appropriate procedures for implementing simple rural buildings could make a very worthwhile contribution to meeting basic human needs, the main issue for the industry remains that of organizing urban construction, more sophisticated building works and civil engineering projects generally. Professional design skills will continue to be necessary, and the practical execution of projects will continue to require a high level of knowledge and experience. Since scarce and expensive national resources are at stake, it is also inevitable that the administration and allocation of finance and physical resources will continue to be planned and controlled centrally. So designers, contractors and administrators will still be needed; what is worth considering is whether the existing highly compartmentalized contractual system is the best way of developing their skills and resources.

Designers and administrators, with well-regarded academic

qualifications and high status, can usually take care of themselves. But domestic contractors in developing countries have rarely achieved a comparable degree of acceptance to that of expatriate firms in their home environment. The explanation is largely historical. Contractors in countries like the United Kingdom were a power in their own right while the institutional framework was taking shape and, in a classical British compromise, were content to trade an inferior legal status for a good deal of *de facto* power arising from their growing financial and technical strength. They also learnt the advantages of working together in a trade association. As early as 1834 a small group of the leading master builders in London formed The Builders' Society to 'uphold and promote reputable standards of building through friendly intercourse, the useful exchange of information and greater uniformity and respectability in building'.

Unfortunately for the developing country domestic contractors when they eventually appeared on the scene, the rule book had been written and they had few weapons with which to negotiate an equitable share in the industry of which they sought to be a part. We referred in Chapter 2 to the perception of a typical developing country contractor as an 'unpatriotic, dishonest businessman'. In truth, contractors, like most groups of human beings, tend to act in accordance with the public perception of their behaviour; however good or bad, however accurately or inaccurately understood.

The ancient Scottish adage suggests that having given 'a dog a bad name' the next step is to 'hang him.' Certainly these contractors have been strung up with a succession of strict contractual obligations which severely inhibit their capacity to compete effectively in their home markets. No doubt clients can point to bad experiences, but unfortunately these obligations do not discriminate between the *bona fide* contractor eager to obtain work and properly execute it, and those with more dubious objectives. Moreover, the contractors with good technical skills and a serious disposition generally do not have the financial and managerial ability to cope with them. In an over-zealous attempt, therefore, to ensure that only 'good' contractors are allowed to survive, developing country governments often militate against the growth of the very contractors who could provide the foundation of an effective domestic sector.

Our analysis so far suggests that a major factor in the generally disappointing performance of indigenous contractors in developing countries has been their powerlessness as individual enterprises to regulate critical transactions across the boundary with the operating environment. *In short they have not had too much power, but too little.* Risks have been multiplied, both deliberately by imposing strict legal and financial clauses in the conditions of contract and—as things have often worked out in practice—by bureaucratic supervision procedures and irregular delays in honouring payment certificates. Thus the cards have effectively been stacked against the contractor before he gets to the table.

So what should be done about the domestic contractor and his inadequate performance? The usual response of government (which, after all, is in the regulatory business!) is to introduce still tighter controls in order to induce these recalcitrants to mend their ways. Although this may be seen as a 'natural' response it is evident that the tightening of controls from outside reduces the authority and accountability of the management of the enterprise and endangers its viability: thus the effect of imposing additional controls may be quite the opposite of what was intended.

This is not to say that loosening of controls will of itself automatically increase efficiency. Naturally, the integrity and competence of management are also important factors. However, the fewer the constraints that are imposed, the more possible it becomes to assess the competence with which management exercises its discretion. Incompetent or frivolous contractors can then be identified and removed from tender lists, thereby encouraging the survival of the fittest. Tight constraints, on the other hand, provide a permanent and justifiable alibi for inefficiency and make it dificult to distinguish the competent from the incompetent.

Towards an Equitable Institutional Framework

If the strategy of emancipating, rather than shackling, the domestic contractor is accepted, there will at least be a prospect of engineering an equitable and balanced institutional framework, in which all members of the construction team (not just the designers and administrators) have a chance to contribute towards a more effective industrial effort.

Contracting is a 'lumpy' business, with turnover typically made up of a small number of substantial contracts each of which puts the contractor at risk for a considerable period. Indeed, if the length of the average contract is measured by the time which elapses from bidding to receipt of the final payment, the simplest construction transaction lasts for over a year and far exceeds that for the typical trader or manufacturer. The lumpiness of contracting makes it an even more risky business for the neophyte. There are numerous examples of previously successful firms being forced into liquidation or bankruptcy by a single loss-making contract, and the temptation for the inexperienced contractor to 'buy work' by bidding low when his order book declines is hard to resist.

Since clients and their professional advisers want comparable bids, they rarely welcome suggestions from the tenderers on alternative approaches to meeting the design requirements despite (or perhaps because of) the contractors' probably superior knowledge of practical construction techniques. The conditions of contract, transferring every possible risk to the contractor, are hardly ever negotiable, even if the contractor could offer a more favourable price structure in return for a less exposed contractual position.

Does the client really gain by transferring all risks to the contractor? In industrialized countries, where contractors can evaluate risks accurately and have the resources to take the rough with the smooth, the answer can be a guarded 'yes' (although even this could be disputed). In developing countries anxious to encourage their fragile domestic industries, excessive risk transference is definitely counter-productive. Yet there is nothing truly sacrosanct about the current risk spread between client and contractor (even if most professionals continue to make daily obeisance to it). A few brave iconoclasts are to be found, and as we have seen the World Bank team, which set out to produce a framework for the promotion of domestic construction industries in developing countries, made the following proposals.[1] These were that, in the initial stages of development, risk transference should be limited by:

(i) The client accepting responsibility for damage to the works resulting from natural causes.
(ii) The client being responsible for investigating and guaranteeing sub-surface conditions.
(iii) The contractor being relieved of the responsibility of advising the client of deficiencies in the drawings.
(iv) Penalties for late completion being small; and even.
(v) Relieving the contractor of responsibility for non-wilful negligence.

There has been no experimentation with these suggestions, so the would-be developing country contractor remains at the mercy of a formidable array of endemic and imposed risks that he is frequently unable to understand, let alone evaluate. The client, meanwhile, continues to decide on which bid is most favourable on price grounds alone, providing that he is satisfied that the bidder is financially solvent and offers to complete within the desired contract period. Accordingly it is only in the financial area that any effective discretion is available to the contractor at the bidding stage. Even this discretion is effectively limited for neophyte bidders by the problems they experience in mastering the somewhat esoteric estimating techniques that are demanded by the traditional system incorporating a bill of quantities.

Could there be a better way? Little research[2] has been done on alternative approaches but, providing designs were fixed with reasonable certainty in advance (and the contractor supplied a schedule of rates to cope with minor variations) some compromise should be possible. In the absence of research a definitive suggestion is not possible, but most developing country contractors would be happier to price a tender document that conformed more closely to their methodology, and split the project into their four major cost elements of materials, labour, plant and overheads. Such a document might take the form set out on page 116.

The contractor would be able to take his profit either through individual materials, labour and plant items, or as a percentage within overheads. There would generally be no need for remeasurement of a contract under such a system and a contractor who, through poor management, used excessive materials, labour or plant would bear the loss himself as at present (equally, benefits from savings would accrue wholly to the contractor). The application of price escalation clauses in countries with high inflation would be distinctly easier than at present, as the appropriate percentage adjustment could be made directly to individual items (or groups of items) according to the set quantity of materials or the contractor's estimate of duration in the cases of labour or plant.

A contractor can save costly accounting time by integrating estimating and costing procedures, and thereby make use of the initial estimate as a yardstick against which to measure actual costs. Thus sophisticated contractors have learnt to distort their costing systems to suit the layout of the conventional bill of quantities,

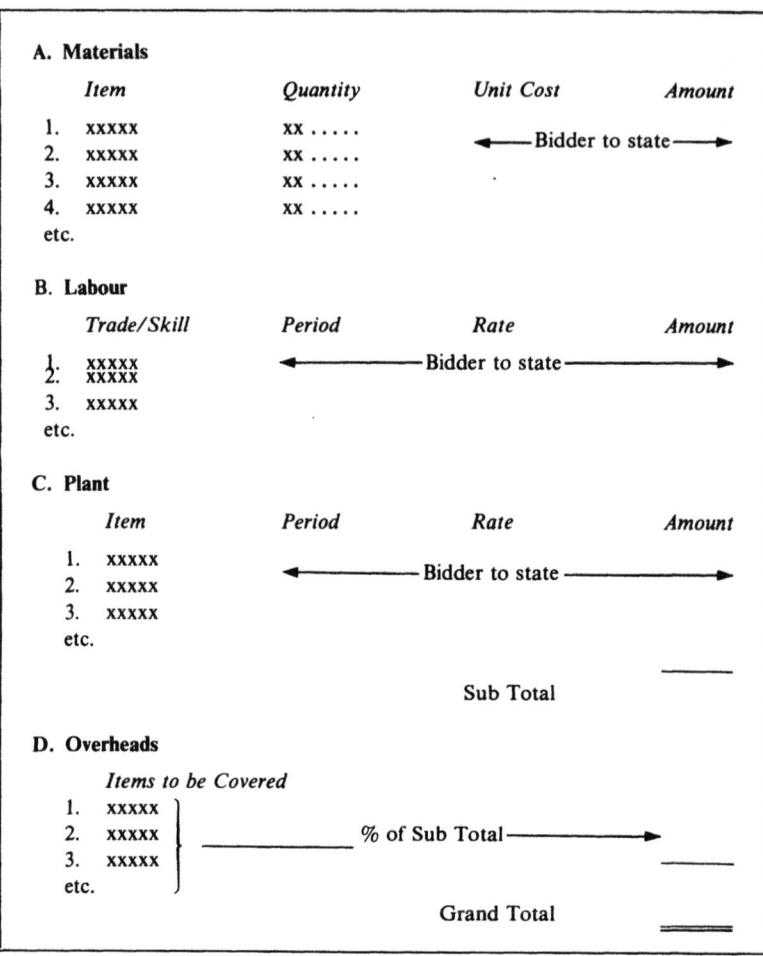

although this is not really practical for a contractor without a strong financial orientation. Deliberately contractor-oriented tender systems of the kind suggested above would help to offset this competitive disadvantage by providing a set of clear cost targets with the key resources of materials, labour, plant and over-heads separately identified, rather than lost in a morass of artificial items.

The Concept of Contractor Development Agencies

The above example shows one way of changing one aspect of the framework in order to release the constraints presently imposed upon the contractor. Unfortunately, however, any major change will only be brought about by the concerted action of those involved in the industry—client, consultant and contractor.

Clients (usually governments) might ponder the possibility of modifying the framework that governs the industry in a way that will deliberately encourage the emergence of capable and well-motivated domestic construction businesses. How can this be done? Entrepreneurial development is a delicate operation, as assistance must be delivered in a way that bolsters self-reliance rather than dependence. However, some brave governments—notably Kenya with its National Construction Corporation—have set up institutions with the deliberate intent of strengthening their domestic construction industries.[3] We will give such institutions the generic title Contractor Development Agencies (CDA's), and the remainder of this chapter will put forward some criteria which may help decision-makers to take the experiment a stage further.

An essential feature of the CDA concept is that it should have sufficient autonomy to be in a position to gain the trust of both contractors and their clients. It will of course have to maintain close

Figure 5. Criteria for Contractor Development Agency

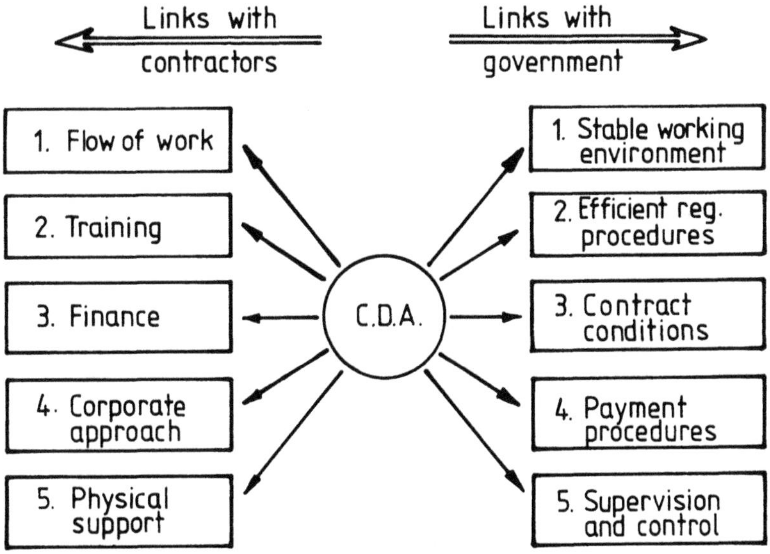

Links with contractors		Links with government
1. Flow of work		1. Stable working environment
2. Training		2. Efficient reg. procedures
3. Finance	C.D.A.	3. Contract conditions
4. Corporate approach		4. Payment procedures
5. Physical support		5. Supervision and control

links with the government and will be financed within the public sector, but its Board of Directors should preferably include some non-government appointees so that it can also be seen by the domestic contractors as their agent with the ear of government. The perception of the CDA as an intermediary is fundamental, and its potential links with both contractors and government are illustrated in Fig. 5.

Links with contractors

These links will aim to strengthen the capacity of the domestic construction industry to a stage where it is broadly self-sufficient. Five main types of support are possible, although the chosen mix will depend on the stage of development, national priorities and the availability of funds:

(i) *Flow of work*: Abrupt fluctuations in workload bedevil the commercial operations of most developing country contractors, since they inhibit a serious commitment to the industry and render investment in improved capacity uneconomic. The CDA can help to even out these peaks and troughs by acting as a channel through which government contracts are directed to domestic contractors. As in the case of Kenya's NCC it may be helpful to utilize some form of main contractor/sub-contractor relationship to safeguard the interests of both the CDA and the ultimate client. There are three drawbacks to this form of support. Firstly, the mechanism for choosing which firms to assist must be made as objective as possible, which is not easy in the face of political and other pressures. Secondly, the CDA will require sufficient qualified staff to review bids put forward by domestic contractors, negotiate contracts on their behalf and supervise work in progress to ensure that contract deadlines are met. Thirdly, although contractual risks can be passed on by the CDA to its subcontractor, a financial reserve will be required to cope with occasional defaults. Despite these drawbacks, and the costs which they entail, this remains a powerful and effective form of support since it permits the businesses concerned to plan and invest with reasonable confidence that the consequent overheads will be recoverable.

(ii) *Training*: All the experience shows that the main need is for training in basic construction management. To return to our previous discussion, it will only be possible to take advantage of releasing the constraints if there is management skill available to deal with the interface between the enterprise and its environment. In developing countries most contractors are essentially practical men, who may have experienced trade or vocational training but are very unlikely to have received any formal management training. The problem is that, although inadequate construction management expertise is a very serious constraint on performance, the deficiency is not always appreciated by those who suffer from it. Thus the task for trainers is not only to organize delivery channels for appropriate training, but also to sell the idea and devise forms of presentation which will make training attractive and demonstrably relevant. It is also helpful to link training to other forms of support to ensure full motivation of the participants. Training content will vary. In general, the approach for the category of owners and general managers will be to assist them in giving an insight into strategic planning and control, with emphasis on costing, estimating and tendering, financial management, commercial and legal aspects, personnel management, the economics of plant operation, purchasing procedures and office administration. For site managers the emphasis will be on topics such as site layout, planning and control of site operations, documentation and basic costing, plant performance and operation, human relations, safety and welfare. Training, although identified as a separate form of support, should of course be implicit in all the CDA's operations. It should also be obligatory for those who benefit, by obtaining contracts, from the work of the CDA.

(iii) *Finance*: Finance can take the form of short-term assistance with working capital needs and/or longer term financing of physical assets. Provision of contract bonds and guarantees is also a very valuable service, since the charges and collateral requirements imposed by banks or insurance companies are a severe burden for the undercapitalized contractor. Preferably financial assistance should be provided in association with an experienced local banking institution, and careful thought must be given to setting interest rates and collateral requirements. Terms should be sufficiently soft to allow the contractor to accumulate funds for expansion, but there is also a need to inculcate financial discipline and discourage speculation.

(iv) *Corporate approach*: The CDA should aim to foster a corporate approach to solving domestic contractors' problems by stimulating the formation of contractors' federations and carrying out general public relations for the industry. This is a delicate matter, since the CDA should aim to encourage the contractors to help themselves by gradually withdrawing from its leading role. Thus the need is for a very sensitive approach by CDA staff so that the contractors' federation is accepted as a genuine voice of the industry, negotiating with the government on topics of mutual interest such as training or contract conditions, rather than degenerating into a restrictive cartel.

(v) *Physical support*: Domestic contractors are frequently at a disadvantage in acquiring plant and materials, since their finances and trading records are rarely strong enough to encourage dealers to open significant lines of credit. Thus there are attractions in permitting a CDA to provide physical support to contractors, such as a pool of plant for hire or the bulk purchase of materials. Such services must be strictly controlled and the services should preferably become self-financing over a period, both to limit the cost and to encourage contractors to become self-reliant when they have accumulated sufficient resources and experience.

CDA links with government
These links will aim to assist government to formulate policies and procedures that will be conducive to the development of a competent and effective domestic contracting industry. Whilst not subverting the negotiating efforts of the contractors' federation, the CDA should be in a uniquely favourable position to mediate between the legitimate concerns of clients and contractors in the national interest. As a parastatal it should be able to secure the confidence of other public sector bodies, and should be acceptable as a technically competent, but disinterested, intermediary in formulating detailed proposals in the following five areas:

(i) *Stable working environment*: Discontinuity in the flow of contracts available for bidding bears particularly heavily on ambitious local firms who aim to build up an inventory of appropriate equipment and maintain a steady well-trained work force. Whilst one approach, discussed earlier, is for projects to be channelled through the CDA (as with the SLCC in Sri Lanka), a less costly (although perhaps less effective) alternative is for it to attempt to persuade public sector clients to co-ordinate their building programmes so as to engineer a steadier flow of work. Although some seasonal and cyclical variations are inevitable, it is sometimes possible to iron out the most severe peaks and troughs without any serious delay to the implementation of development plans. Another possibility is to 'cut and slice' large projects to provide a number of smaller contracts for which domestic contractors could bid within their available resources.

(ii) *Efficient registration procedures*: Although fully-open tendering may appear to give the client the benefits of keener pricing due to maximum competition, a better overall service can be secured by inviting bids from a selected list of qualified firms. Since it would be too expensive and time-consuming to practice contract-by-contract pre-qualification procedures on other than large and specialized projects, this can be most conveniently achieved on the basis of a graded register of qualified contractors. This system will only be effective if registration procedures are thorough, including inspection to check that data provided by the applicant is correct, and gradings must be regularly updated and reviewed. Once the register is in operation, projects up to a certain value can be closed to foreign contractors and percentage preferences can be allowed to domestic contractors bidding for projects in grades above this limit. Furthermore, 'downward plundering' can be eliminated by seeking bids only from contractors within the appropriate grades. A secondary benefit from an efficient registration system is that a contractor is more likely to build up his resources and make a genuine effort to satisfy his clients' requirements if he knows that his progress is being regularly monitored.

(iii) *Contract conditions*: In several countries the authors have encountered conditions of contract, specifications and standard designs that act as a positive disincentive to domestic contractors. A tendency to specify imported products, coupled with foreign exchange restrictions that bear more heavily on domestic firms, results in a powerful hidden competitive advantage for foreign contractors. Foreign contractors also usually have more experience in negotiating additional payments for contract variations, and have better access to banking and insurance sources to meet restrictive bonding and guarantee requirements.

(iv) *Payment procedures*: Erratic payment procedures bear particularly heavily on the undercapitalized domestic contractor and a CDA could have a significant impact in assisting ministries and other public sector client organizations to streamline payment procedures so that contractors can rely upon a steadier cash flow. In turn, the clients will eventually benefit from more competitive tenders as contractors reduce the risk premium that they include in overheads to defray anticipated delays in settlement.

(v) *Supervision and control*: The CDA can also act as a useful intermediary between contractors and their clients in ensuring fair, consistent and effective supervision and quality control. Most contract documents leave a great deal of discretion to architects, engineers and clerks-of-works to decide on an acceptable standard of work. These individuals need considerable experience to strike a fair balance between the aim to produce a quality structure and fair treatment of a contractor working with imperfect materials in difficult circumstances.

Balance, judgement and sensitivity
Like any other group of tightrope walkers, the staff of a CDA require the qualities of balance, judgement and sensitivity. It will not be easy to maintain a basic autonomy and balance between links with contractors and clients in the face of contradictory pressures, but this is essential in order to minimize suspicion by both groups. A further requirement is a power to discriminate between contractors in the provision of a flow of work and financial or other assistance. Ensuring that such discrimination is based on objective criteria, and is seen to be free from political or other interference, will inevitably give rise to considerable difficulties. But the alternative is to court popularity by spreading assistance so thinly that it is bound to be ineffective, and the result may in fact be counter-productive in attracting additional poorly-motivated speculators into what is already an overcrowded industry. The quality of sensitivity will be paramount in the staff's dealings with its domestic contractor clients.

The requirement is to help contractors without making them over-dependent. Thus CDA site supervisors must be careful never to issue orders direct to the contractor's staff, or to negotiate directly with the client, but always work through the contractor or his representative. It is vital that all CDA staff recognize and remember that their role is essentially one of training and upgrading the contractors with whom they are working, and their job descriptions and working practices must reflect this.

What will it cost? The problem of financing a CDA can be met in a variety of ways. Aid organizations and international agencies may be prepared to provide technical assistance and other support in the early stages, but there will inevitably be some call for local financing. This can come directly from a central budget allocation, or funds can be raised (directly or indirectly) from the industry. Indirect financing can be secured on the levy/grant principle, as practised by such organizations as the British Construction Industry Training Board or the Nigerian Industrial Training Fund. Direct financing can be raised by charging participating firms for services rendered, including loan interest, bond and guarantee fees, course fees, consultancy and supervision charges, plant hire payments and charges for procurement of materials. An element of direct financing is desirable since this provides a measure of the real demand for CDA services, allows rationing by price when resources are scarce, and encourages the contractor to build up his own capacity in order to reduce his outlay on the purchase of CDA services.

Will it ever end? 'Institution building' has become a popular pastime among development agencies, but costly bureaucracies are easier to create than to kill. How can one defeat the inevitable desire of any public sector bureaucracy to achieve self-perpetuation? This is a problem which should be carefully considered by policy-makers before setting up any kind of CDA, but particularly one that is likely to employ significant numbers of staff. One possible solution is to limit the duration from the start, and deliberately employ only expatriates (who can be sent home) and local staff on secondment (who can be sent back to their parent institutions). A variation is to set the CDA the conscious task of 'working itself out of a job' as its domestic contractor clients reach set levels of resources and achievement, and perhaps recruit the demonstrably successful CDA staff onto their own establishments. If this happy ending is too much to hope for, an alternative strategy is to structure the budget of the CDA on the basis of a steadily declining annual subsidy which will have to be augmented by a steadily increasing revenue from direct charges on participating firms. The objective in this case would be for the CDA to eventually turn itself into a self-financing service organization on the lines of the United Kingdom's Building Advisory Service (BAS).

Staffing The questions of financing and the ultimate destination of the CDA are crucial to the motivation of CDA staff, and salaries in excess of normal civil service pay scales may be necessary to attract high calibre staff with the rare blend of theoretical knowledge and practical experience that is needed to gain the respect of hard-headed entrepreneurs. The CDA must beware of the dangers of settling into a comfortable rut. Staffing it with personnel seconded from other institutions would be a way of encouraging a regular input of new ideas and enthusiasm. The key appointment is that of General Manager, since this individual will need to devote a great deal of time and effort to establishing the credibility of the institution, which should produce the beneficial side effect of attracting keen and well-motivated staff.

The way forward

The standard solution to the problems of the construction industry in developing countries is to pump more money in. Given the complexity of the problems and the general lack of understanding of them, it is not surprising that the outcome has frequently proved disappointing. The foregoing paragraphs offer some tentative suggestions for an alternative way forward through the formation of specific contractor development agencies. The concept of the CDA is not presented as a panacea but as a potential channel and catalyst for effective action. Specific proposals would have to be put together to meet the needs of individual countries, and these will vary according to the socio-economic structure, policy priorities and the state of development of the domestic industry. How it has been utilized in one country, Kenya, is described on page 127. The CDA itself, however, is likely to form only a part of an array of measures needed, the object of which is to steadily transform the national construction environment so that it favours the development of a compact and efficient domestic industry.

Up until very recently, the ideas presented in this chapter received limited acceptance. Work carried out in the last 2–3 years by both the ILO and the World Bank, however, has reflected, and indeed developed upon, these concepts.[3,4,5] The ILO, in particular, in its *Guidelines for the development of small-scale contractors*[4] has mapped out a detailed scenario showing how a contractor development agency might assist in the promotion of a healthy domestic construction sector. The *Guidelines* rightly point out that the CDA would take different forms depending upon the particular socio-economic and political environment. They also recognize the main argument of this book that, for any effective development to take place, the institutional procedures of the industry must be geared to assist rather than inhibit the neophyte contractor.

An efficient contractual system would attempt to ensure that output is maximized and cost minimized, whilst ensuring that each party in the process perceives that his objectives are at least partially realized.

The question that one has to ask is whether the existing contractual system actually does this. The evidence suggests that it does not. This stems from the fact that the system is generally used to constrain and limit the contractor even though it is he who actually executes the work. Unfortunately, in an attempt to ensure that the contractor works efficiently by imposing restraining conditions upon him, the system automatically produces its own inefficiency.

We have argued that a more efficient domestic contracting sector, supported by governments, provides the basis for reaping long-term benefits to the economy and the country as a whole. An efficient contract is one in which both parties are satisfied with the result. Thus, any so-called improvement must yield satisfaction to both client and contractor and, in the long run, this can only be achieved by creating a more appropriate industrial framework.

In the short term it will, of course, be necessary to provide training to indigenous contractors. Whatever the framework, it is clear that many lack the ability to carry out the basic tasks of resource planning, estimating and tendering, and site management. Nevertheless, training in isolation is not of great value; it must be carried out on the foundation of overall support to the domestic sector. There must be a catalytic entity which can provide a channel of communication between client and contractor, and which can be seen to be working in the interests of both parties.

This process will take time. Most CDA proposals cannot be expected to show a measurable return in less than five years, and the Kenya NCC still foresees an important range of tasks after 17 years. In some countries, this will be taken as an excuse for inertia, on the grounds that the problems are here and now, and there is no spare time to worry about the medium and longer term. The result is that, over the years, these countries continue to be at the mercy of a high cost industry of limited efficiency, often dependent on expensive foreign resources and skills, and with no prospect of change for the better. While the problems are daunting, we believe that the opportunities are attractive and stimulating, while the rewards will far outweigh the risks for those countries with the courage to act.

Annex The Kenya National Construction Corporation— A CDA in Practice*

Several governments (including Ghana and Sri Lanka) have taken sporadic initiatives to assist their domestic construction industries, but there are only a few examples of attempts at a comprehensive and integrated approach to construction industry development. The most sustained and successful of these is the Kenya National Construction Corporation Ltd. (NCC), which was started as a joint venture between the Kenya Government and NORAD (the Norwegian aid agency) in 1967. The NCC—now fully Kenyanized apart from three middle rank technical advisers among a total staff of 250—provides support to domestic contractors in three main ways:

(i) Allocation and supervision of Government and other contracts.
(ii) Training and educational facilities.
(iii) Short-term loan finance to provide working capital.

In short the Corporation is a combination of 'contractor', 'school' and 'bank.' This may seem an odd combination, but it means that the NCC is in a position to provide integrated support with both formal and 'on-the-job' training linked to continuity of work and financial assistance. What is more, although its performance in delivering this support has been patchy, it seems to have worked. There were few African contractors at the time of independence (1963), and those few were small and scattered, scraping a living from minor building projects, materials haulage and 'labour-only' sub-contracting.

This deficiency was rapidly appreciated by the new government, which announced in its Five-Year Development Plan 1965-9 that it was preparing to establish a body (the NCC), the principal objective of which was to bring African contractors into the construction industry. The main barriers facing African contracting firms were described as:

... lack of knowledge of managerial and commercial administrative matters, inexperience in site organization, insufficient financial

---

* This Annex is based on National Construction Corporation of Kenya, 'An approach to the development of an indigenous construction industry' *Construction Management Case* No. 1 (Geneva, ILO, 1979).

means, including difficulties in obtaining credit from suppliers of materials, and inadequate plant and transportation equipment.

The barriers remain formidable but, at least within the building sub-sector upon which the NCC has focussed its attention over the last 15 years, they have been breached by significant numbers of active and determined local firms. There were in 1982 six African citizen contractors accepted by the Ministry of Works and Housing as competent to bid for building contracts of Kshs 15 million (US$1·5 million) and above, and five of these are regarded as capable of executing work at the highest level of job complexity (intricate foundations, reinforced concrete structures, etc.). For building projects in excess of Kshs 5 million there is a group of ten indigenous firms, rising to 27 and 74 for projects in excess of 2 and 1 million shillings respectively.

Most fair-minded observers agree that, unaided, African contractors would not have been able to achieve anything like this degree of penetration of their construction market. A more formidable criticism concerns the expense of running the organization, which is now running close to Kshs 10 million ($1 million) per annum. However, about half of this is recovered from income on loan charges and interest, bond fees, plant hire, rental income and management and supervision fees. Furthermore, there is the real, albeit hard to measure, benefit to the nation resulting from the now substantial pool of indigenous contractors from whom bids can be sought for a wide range of medium-sized building projects throughout the country.

The NCC was originally established as a limited company, wholly government-owned, under the control of the Ministry of Works. In 1972, it was reorganized and given greater autonomy as a parastatal organization under an Act of Parliament with the continuing objective 'to promote, assist, and develop the construction industry'. The Corporation is run by a Board of Directors appointed by the Minister of Works and Housing, including *ex officio* the Permanent Secretaries of the Ministries of Works, Housing (recently merged), the Treasury, and Commerce and Industry. The Board in turn appoints a General Manager to run the Corporation on its behalf, but has in practice always taken a close interest (through a subcommittee) in sensitive issues like the allocation of loans and contracts.

One of the most interesting aspects of the NCC is its early

recognition of the need to stimulate the formation of an association of indigenous contractors, so as to encourage self-reliance and a realization of their need for collective action to represent their views to the government, and thereby gradually secure a more equitable trading environment. This is a major conceptual step for any paternalistic institution. It takes real imagination and courage to understand and accept the objective of enfranchizing as well as 'helping' one's clients, with the risk (which turned out to be well-founded) that the enfranchized clients may end up criticizing certain aspects of the operations of the institution that encouraged them to get together and make their views known.

The Kenya Association of African Contractors (KAAC) was formed in 1968, a year after the NCC itself, as a channel of communication between African contractors as a group and the NCC, the Ministry of Works and government generally. The Chairman of the KAAC is a member of the Board of Directors of the NCC and the Association has its headquarters in the NCC offices in Nairobi, although there are also seven provincial offices with their own branch committees.

Criticism was voiced by the contractors that the NCC acts more as a supervisor than as a partner. This has always been a sensitive issue, although its Technical Section was always intended to 'accompany the contractor and guide him until he can stand on his own feet'. For, while the NCC's clear objective was to develop the local industry, it also had to remember its fiduciary relationship with those who commissioned projects arising from its role as a 'wholesaler' of building contracts (taking on work in bulk and splitting it into more manageable units for execution by domestic contractors). For each project the NCC took over-all responsibility as the main contractor for compliance with quality standards, conditions of contract and the allowable period for completion. The work was then split on a slice-and-package basis among NCC-approved contractors, whose status was that of sub-contractors to the NCC. Payments on interim and final certificates are made to the NCC as main contractor, and are then passed on to the 'sub-contractor' subject to deductions for bond and management fees, instalments of principal and interest on outstanding loans.

Clearly the NCC had many good things to offer: jobs, bonds and guarantees, finance and plant hire at preferential rates. The message spread quickly, leading to an embarrassing need to restrict the number of NCC-approved contractors in order to ensure continuity of work and effective entrepreneurial development in the face of political pressures to spread the benefits thinly and widely. This dilemma has never been squarely faced. The NCC Annual Report for the years 1967/8 and 1968/9 warned that:

> ... every increase in the number of new contractors should take place as and when they may be absorbed within the frame of overall development, and the list of approved contractors [at that time 46] should be extended very slowly and with due consideration of every applicant.

Nevertheless, by 1971 over 700 firms had been accepted after filling in a short application form and, although attempts were then made to select a 'top 20' and later a 'top 56' group for continuous employment, this policy crumbled as a result of intense pressure from the KAAC. The Corporation's difficulties encountered in trying to provide continuous work to a group of the more promising African contractors have been the most intransigent. A reliable workload is essential if any businessman is to plan his development and recoup longer-term investments in skill upgrading and improved plant and equipment. The result of spreading the available work too thinly is to provide a 'taste' of the contracting industry to a large number of aspirants, and thereby stimulate even fiercer competition for those firms with the potential to become serious and committed contractors. A side effect is that the training and advisory services offered by the NCC (usually free-of-charge) have unfortunately never enjoyed the same popularity as those services that offer the prospect of immediate and tangible profit.

Despite its problems, the NCC remains the most comprehensive and sustained example of a contractor support agency in Africa (and probably elsewhere). The only other two notable examples are the Botswana Enterprises Development Unit (BEDU) and the Swaziland Small Enterprise Development Corporation (SEDCO), both of which are much smaller and more limited in their objectives. The NCC, as a pioneer, has taught useful lessons on both the possibilities and the pitfalls. It has bravely attempted to grasp the former and sidestep the latter.

References

CHAPTER 1

1. G. A. Edmonds, 'The construction industry in developing countries', in *International Labour Review* (Geneva, ILO, May–June 1979).
2. See F. Moavanzadeh, *The role and contribution of the construction industry to socio-economic growth of the developing countries* (prepared for UNCHS, November 1980).
3. See D. A. Turin et al, 'Construction and development: a framework for research and action', a paper prepared for the IBRD (London, University College Environmental Research Group, 1972).
   See also G. A. Edmonds, 'The construction industry in developing countries', op. cit.
4. UCERG Construction and Development, 'A framework for research and action', a paper prepared for IBRD (London, May 1972).
5. J. Rossow and F. Moavanzadeh, *The construction industry in developing countries* (MIT, Spring 1975).
6. R. Neo, *International construction contracting* (Gower Press, 1976).
7. S. Drewer, 'Institutional constraints to the choice of appropriate construction technology', mimeographed *World Employment Programme Research Working Paper*, restricted (Geneva, ILO, December 1982).
8. Author's own estimates.
9. ILO, Building, Civil Engineering and Public Works Committee, *General Report* (Geneva, 1971).
10. J. Capt and G. A. Edmonds, 'Study of small contractors in Kenya', mimeographed *World Employment Programme Research Working Paper*, restricted (Geneva, ILO, December 1977).
11. UN Economic Commission for Africa, *Survey of economic conditions in Africa, 1971* (New York, 1972).
12. UNECA, *A review of the building materials industry in Africa and the possibilities for a rapid expansion* (July 1967).

CHAPTER 2

1. Sir H. Banwell et al, *The placing and management of contracts for building and civil engineering works* (London, HMSO, 1964).
2. J. Bowyer, *History of building* (London, Crosby Lockwood Staples, 1973).
3. L. T. C. Rolt, *Isambard Kingdom Brunel* (Longmans, Green, 1957).

4 J. Capt and G. Edmonds, 'Small contractors in Kenya', mimeographed *World Employment Programme Research Working Paper*, restricted (Geneva, ILO, 1978).
5 G. W. Irvin, *Roads and redistribution—social costs and benefits of labour-intensive road construction in Iran* (Geneva, ILO, 1975).
6 C. K. Johri and S. M. Pandey, *Employment relationship in the building industry* (India, Shri Ram Centre, 1972).
7 G. Ofori, 'The construction industry in Ghana', mimeographed *World Employment Programme Working Paper*, restricted (Geneva, ILO, December 1981).
8 World Bank, *Bangladesh—a review of the construction industry* (Washington, 1978).
9 World Bank, 'A framework for the promotion of construction industries in the developing countries' *Staff Working Paper* No. 168 (November 1973).
10 ILO, 'Study of the role of the private sector in the construction of small rural infrastructure projects in the Philippines'. Report prepared for the ILO by the Development Academy of the Philippines.
11 S. Ganesan, *Management of small construction firms* (Asian Productivity Organisation, Tokyo, 1982.
12 World Bank, *Nepal—a review of the construction industry* (February 1978).
13 PECTA, ILO, Emploi et développement au Cameroun: perspectives sectorielles (Addis Ababa, August 1977).
14 *World Bank Staff Working Paper* 168, op.cit.
15 *World Bank Staff Working Paper* 168, op.cit.
16 *World Bank Staff Working Paper* 168, op.cit.
17 World Bank, February 1978, op.cit.
18 FIDIC, *Inquiry into use of Conditions of Contract (International) for works of civil engineering construction.*
19 World Bank, *Staff Working Paper* 168, op.cit.
20 Clause 60 of the FIDIC Conditions of Contract (International) state that 'payments (to the contractor) shall be made at monthly intervals'. In most developing countries this would be the exception rather than the rule.
21 World Bank, op.cit.
22 World Bank, op.cit.
23 Development Academy of the Philippines, op.cit.
24 B. Balkenhol, op.cit.
25 World Bank, op.cit.
26 World Bank, *Staff Working Paper* 168, op.cit.
27 Development Academy of the Philippines, op.cit.
28 G. Ofori, op.cit.

CHAPTER 3

1 Government of Ghana, *Five Year Development Plan 1975–80, Part I* (Accra, 1977).

2 Government of the Gold Coast, *The Development Plan 1951—being a plan for the economic and social development of the Gold Coast 1951-6* (Accra, 1951).
3 Government of Ghana, *Seven-Year Development Plan, Annual Plan for the Second Plan Year 1965* (Office of the Planning Commission, Accra, 1965).
4 Government of Ghana, *The Budget Statement 1974-5* (Accra, 1974).
5 Government of Ghana, *The Budget Statement 1978-9* (Accra, 1978).
6 Economic Commission for Europe, *Long-Term Prospects and Policies in the Construction Sector* (New York, United Nations, 1976).
7 Pianim, K. A., Chief Executive of Cocoa Marketing Board, in an interview under the heading: 'Ghana's Cocoa', *Daily Graphic*, 22 March 1979.
8 Architectural and Engineering Services Corporation, *The Consultant* (House Journal of AESC), Vol. 2, No. 1.
9 'Why, Oh Why Cement Factory?', *Daily Graphic*, 18 May 1979.
10 Supreme Military Council, *Budget Statement for Fiscal Year 1978-79* (Accra, Ministry of Finance, 1978).
11 See, for example, Jones, T., *Ghana's First Republic 1960-6* (London, Methuen, 1976).
12 Ministry of Works and Housing, AESC, 'Registration of Contractors: Notes for the Guidance of Applicants', Form ROC.2A.
13 Government of Ghana, *Bank for Housing and Construction Decree*, NRCD 135 (1972).
14 Marian Bowley, *The British Building Industry*.
15 Government of Ghana, *One-Year Development Plan, July 1970-June 1971* (Accra, 1970).

CHAPTER 4

1 R. Pennant-Rea, 'Island in a hurry: Sri Lanka—a survey', *The Economist* (13 June 1981).
2 Report of the State Engineering Corporation Review Committee, *Sessional Paper* No. 1, 1973, (Department of Government Printing, March 1973).
3 Report of the Committee of Inquiry into the Present Position of the RVDB with special reference to its Finances (mimeo, Ministry of Lands, Land Development and Mahaweli Development, 1979).
4 Ministry of Planning and Employment, *Five-Year Plan 1972-76* (1971).

CHAPTER 5

1 World Bank, 'A framework for the promotion of construction industries in the Developing Countries', *Staff Working Paper* No. 168 (November 1973).
2 A notable exception is the work of M. Barnes at UMIST.

3 See, for example, Colin Relf, *Helping towards self-reliance: an analysis of government-sponsored assistance to small-scale contracting enterprises in Kenya, Swaziland and Botswana* (ILO, October 1981).
4 ILO, *Guidelines for the development of small-scale contractors* (Geneva, May 1983).
5 World Bank, *The construction industry in developing countries* draft, mimeo (December 1982).

Appendix

Some Lessons from Other ILO Studies

The two case studies contained in Chapters 3 and 4 provide the basis for the arguments developed in Chapter 5. They are detailed, and are developed around the major theme that it is the institutional factors which constrain the growth of domestic construction capacity in developing countries. The ILO has, in addition, carried out other, less comprehensive studies of the industry. This appendix summarizes the results of three of these studies, and in particular how they support the main argument of the book.

West Africa[1]

The first of these studies was carried out by B. Balkenhol as part of the comprehensive employment strategy missions to Niger, Sierra Leone and the United Republic of Cameroon.

In economic terms, the construction industry in all three countries is quite similar, and fits reasonably into the framework described in Chapter 1. Its contribution to GDP is between 3 and 4 per cent in all three countries, which is what one could expect for Niger and Sierra Leone although somewhat low for the United Republic of Cameroon. Employment in the industry varies from 2·4 per 1000 population in Niger to 6·6 in Sierra Leone. This is fairly low by any standard, and particularly so for the United Republic of Cameroon given its level of development. Construction output varies enormously between the three countries in its distribution, reflecting different political and economic goals. As one has grown to expect, most building materials are imported in all three countries. Similarly the industry is dominated by a small number of foreign or foreign-owned firms. The general situation is therefore of heavy investment by government in an industry which does not have the absorptive capacity to take such investment.

There is a lack of domestic capacity in all three countries. There is just one local, qualified, civil engineer in Niger in the whole of the

Table A   The industry in three West African countries.

	GNP per capita ($)	Value added as % of GDP	Employment per 1,000 pop.	Value added in construction per capita
Niger	330	3·1	2·4	10·0
United Republic of Cameroon	670	3·7	4·5	25·0
Sierra Leone	280	3·0	6·6	8·5

private construction sector. There are very few consulting firms in Sierra Leone, and none at all in Niger. Sub-contracting, a means whereby large firms can at least help to develop smaller firms, is limited in all three countries, amounting to 5–15 per cent of annual turnover.

The structure and the organization of the industry is generally weighted in favour of the large, predominantly foreign-owned firms. In general, there is a restriction on the *maximum* size of contract a contractor can bid for, but there is no minimum. This results in downward plundering by the large contractors when economic conditions are tight, which is most of the time. Thus in the United Republic of Cameroon, category A (large) contractors obtain as much as 75 per cent of the contracts intended for smaller contractors.

The tendering system in all three countries exhibits all the limitations which restrict the growth of the local contractor in most other developing countries. Registration fees, bank guarantees, bid and performance bonds and evidence of previous experience and expertise limit his capacity to obtain and start a contract; lack of credit, slow payment and penalty clauses hamper his chances of making a reasonable profit.

The study also discussed the general question of whether, if there were so many barriers to the development of small contractors, it was worth considering assisting them at all. This is a new way of looking at the problem. Our assumption has been that a healthy private construction sector is a necessity in a mixed economy, and it is a *sine qua non* that the institutional constraints should be released. Balkenhol, however, argues that it is only worth helping them if they are *economically* efficient. He points out that labour productivity is higher in larger firms, and that smaller firms are not necessarily more labour-intensive (as measured by capital/output ratios) than larger ones. He sees, therefore, no *economic* argument for support to the local contractor. He admits, however, that this is a rather limited view and, even in economic terms, does not take account of the long term national interest. Moreover, he accepts that certain products, such as houses, should be reserved for small contractors on the basis that they are a basic need and can therefore be considered as a *social* good which the government should subsidize.

Another interesting aspect of the study was its investigation of the informal sector in Sierra Leone. The small builders interviewed generally employed less than 10 people at any one time, did not always have work, owned some tools and wheelbarrows but rarely a concrete mixer or block-making machine. Of the more successful of the small constructors interviewed the majority had previously worked for a large contractor. They were generally *technically* capable, but not conversant with financial management.

Evidence from the study supports the ideas presented in Chapter 5 that there is a need for a strict screening to identify contractors to be assisted; that effective credit systems must be devised for small contractors; and that the existing procedures must be modified if there is to be any hope of developing a viable domestic contracting sector.

Kenya[2]

The study was carried out at a time (1977) when the Kenyan economy was buoyant. Since that time, coffee and tea prices have declined and the construction sector has suffered along with the rest of the economy. Clearly, therefore, the results of the study relate to a better situation than presently exists vis-à-vis small contractors.

Of the 1,500 construction enterprises in Kenya, nearly two-thirds are one-man firms. At the other extreme, 10 per cent of the firms employ 50 employees or more and account for 82 per cent of those employed in the industry. Firms employing 4 employees or less account for 3 per cent of employment but only 1 per cent of the output of the construction industry. The productivity of the smaller firms (measured as output per worker) is only 50 per cent of the larger ones.

The industry in Kenya provides employment to some 50,000 people, two-thirds of this total on a regular basis. Whilst the overall level of employment is low (3·4 per 1000 population) it is centred on

Nairobi where the majority of workers are employed. Although having only 5 per cent of the country's population, Nairobi provides 50 per cent of construction employment.

In relation to the output of the industry, labour represents 14 per cent of the total, materials 48 per cent, plant 8 per cent and profit and overheads 30 per cent. For the 1,050 smallest firms, i.e. 60 per cent of the total, labour represents 24 per cent of the total output which suggests (a) a low productivity in the small firms (cf. Sierra Leone); and (b) a higher level of labour-intensity. In summary, we can say that the construction industry in Kenya is fairly typical of others in the developing countries. It provides a healthy contribution to the Gross Domestic Product and a major share of the total investment. This investment is mainly in infrastructural works. Private firms account for 70 per cent of the output. The distribution of work and employment, however, is heavily orientated towards the small number of larger firms. These firms tend to use less labour per unit of output than the smaller firms, but they do so more efficiently.

Geographically, there is a major concentration of work in the Nairobi area and, to a much lesser extent, in Mombasa and Nakuru. The densely populated areas in the west of Kenya are, on the other hand, poorly served in terms of construction activity and employment.

As much as 30 per cent of the labour force is employed on a casual basis. The private sector utilizes casual labour less than the public sector, probably reflecting the concentration of private sector work in the urban areas, and the greater impact of trade unions in this sector. Furthermore, major programmes in the public sector such as the Rural Access Roads Programme are based on the employment of the unemployed in the rural areas on a casual basis.

Wages in the private sector are generally higher than in the public sector, again reflecting the concentration of private sector work in the urban areas and the greater impact of the trade unions.

The input of materials, many of which are imported, is high, comprising nearly 50 per cent of the total resource input. Whilst the contribution of equipment to total input is generally quite small it should be recognized that virtually all equipment is imported. Once imported, it is used again and again and requires further capital imports of spare parts.

The small firms use labour to a much greater extent, but they use it less efficiently. The survey covered 97 firms distributed throughout

Kenya. The majority of firms were small, over 60 per cent having fewer than ten employees. Seventy per cent classified themselves as general builders and the majority were relatively young; less than 20 per cent had been in business more than 15 years and as much as 40 per cent were less than 5 years old. The largest firms tended to be limited companies.

The firms often came into existence because the owner had worked in the industry. They, on average, tendered for five or six jobs a year but obtained only two. They did not travel very far to obtain work, the limit being about 10 km from their base.

From the point of view of employment the firms were the contradiction of conventional wisdom regarding small firms in Europe. This is basically due to the use of casual labour to act as a safety valve. Whilst the national ratio of casual to permanent employees employed by construction enterprises was 1 to 2, the smallest firms had a ratio of 6 to 1.

In terms of efficiency the survey reflected the national findings; output per head increases with increasing firm size. The efficiency of using finance may relate to the difficulty of obtaining credit. As Balkenhol found in Sierra Leone, small contractors rarely use institutional means to obtain credit. Furthermore, as Edmonds found in his study on British contractors,[3] small contractors in Kenya live much more precariously in that the ratio of turnover to assets is much higher than for larger firms. This suggests that they are inherently unstable and that a small liquidity problem may cause bankruptcy.

As far as the general running of their business was concerned most of the firms felt that irregularity of payment by the client was their major problem. Many of the firms had to pay for materials in advance, thus exacerbating their liquidity problems.

The survey of small contractors in Kenya in many ways reinforces the commonly held views about the status of small contractors in a developing country. They are caught in a variety of interlocking circles of constraint:

(i) To obtain jobs they have to have fixed assets, to obtain these they need credit, and this is not forthcoming unless they are on a government tender list or have a job.

(ii) They need a reliable permanent labour force to carry out work effectively, they cannot afford a modest permanent staff unless they have some continuity of work, but jobs will only be given to them if they can prove that they have been efficient in the completion of work that they have done.

(iii) To become viable and stable they must increase their fixed assets, but this can only be done if they have sufficient profit to reinvest in the company. Because they have no continuity of work the retained profit is used up in fixed overheads. It is not invested in plant, equipment or permanent staff as they have no assurance that jobs will be available to them.

(iv) The smaller the firm the more it relies on casual labour which is generally unskilled. Consequently, the more likelihood there is that the standard of workmanship is inadequate, which will limit the chances of obtaining further work.

(v) The outflow of cash is fixed at regular intervals by materials suppliers, employees and plant hire companies. However, the inflow is irregular. The cash flow deficit has to be covered from the firms' resources, again limiting the amount that can be reserved for acquisition of fixed assets.

(vi) Small contractors cannot afford, or obtain credit, for the purchase of plant and equipment. They are often trapped in a sequence of inefficient technology, low productivity, low income leading back full circle to inefficient technology.

For domestic contractors in Kenya to break out of these restrictive cycles new initiatives are required. The results of the survey indicated the magnitude of the problem in terms of the viability of the firms themselves. Nevertheless, there are other issues such as training and institutional procedures which also affect the environment in which the contractor works.

Mauritius

Mauritius is an island in the Indian Ocean. It has a population of 940,000 living in an area of 1,865 square kilometres, giving it one of the highest population densities in the world. This population is marked by its ethnic diversity and the fact that 96 per cent live in the main urban centres.

The economy of the island is heavily dependent upon sugar cane, the industry contributing 88 per cent of all agricultural employment.

Sugar accounts for 66 per cent of total exports. At $900 GNP per capita the country cannot be classified as poor. However, its rather peculiar geographic, social and economic situation provides an interesting framework in which to study the construction industry.

Over the last 10 years there has been a relative boom in construction, particularly in housing. In consequence growth of employment in the industry was only exceeded in the manufacturing industry. As far as other inputs are concerned the level of imported materials has increased over recent years. In 1979 construction materials accounted for 8 per cent of all imports, and 80 per cent of these were cement and steel products.

The growth of the industry has not been marked by an increase in Mauritian involvement. Most of the work is carried out by foreign or foreign-owned contractors drawing their technology and construction practices from the modern international model rather than from any attempt to develop an appropriate technology. The limited number of Mauritian architects and engineers are all involved in the modern approach and are often linked to the foreign or foreign-owned firms.

The building regulations (unchanged since 1919) and conditions of contract are based also on a model which has little to do with the Mauritian environment. Not surprisingly, perhaps, the level of ability of locally initiated construction is very low.

The institutional framework which currently exists in Mauritius shows it to be marked by characteristics more pertinent to a developed than a developing country. Also market concentration, even in those areas where indigenous firms and professions have a high profile, is greater than in the 'typical' developed country.

Although a local public authority is formally the client, expatriate agencies fund a significant volume of building and infrastructural work. This limits the role of the local government in initiating new (and more appropriate) construction techniques. A similar situation exists in the private corporate sector, where the local government has only limited power to intervene. The evidence shows that the area where local clients have a greater measure of freedom of choice is in new housing.

Clients who generate independent demand for new housing—mainly those from middle- or upper-income groups—tend to adopt an assumed 'modern' standard of design. New housing with a strong 'social' element is marked by the influence of external agents—funding agencies and designers—in determining building standards and design. This tends to result in building types and techniques being adopted which reflect many of the characteristics of the local middle-income group.

Housing for similar groups produced by the informal, or near-formal, sectors tends to be more liberal in the use of space, concrete and steel. The use of space reflects the demonstration effect in conditioning choice, but the use of an excess of concrete and steel is the result of an awareness that a lower quality of labour and materials are used in the production of this category of housing. Social housing is therefore a hybrid—reflecting local middle-income aesthetics and detailed designs which, although related in many ways to local conditions, are essentially rooted in the social housing programmes of developed countries.

When we consider the possible development of the domestic sector as an instrument of change a similar situation prevails. Mauritius has a few contractors who are competent by international standards. Their technical skills and training are reflected in their management, production techniques and aspirations. They are more labour-intensive than would be similar contractors in a developed country. However this is not simply a reflection of the relative cost of labour, but also a recognition of lower levels of productivity and, in many areas, lower levels of operative skills. Where they do take technical initiatives it is in importing construction equipment and building systems such as precast concrete plants. The pressures they apply—which are quite consistent with their own success criteria—reinforce the pressures to use 'international modern' methods.

Producers and suppliers of building materials and components operate in a similar manner to that of the large local contractors. All the cement used is imported through a major Franco-Mauritian Trading Company; a few similar companies dominate the imports of most other building materials. Some large contractors do however directly import some materials for their own projects. Where a significant local capacity to produce or process building materials does exist—for example in plants, steel bars, ready-mixed concrete and aggregate—production is highly concentrated and firms are usually associates of major trading companies, expatriate concerns or large sugar producers. Again there is a bias towards the use of 'modern' equipment, materials and construction techniques.

The Mauritius study was somewhat more conceptual than the others. The concern was the development of the industry taking appropriate technology into consideration. The conclusions, however, are similar to our own, viz. it requires a major commitment on the part of developing countries to change the rules of such a complex game as construction. When initiating construction programmes, with all their complexities and problems of funding and realization, the tendency to fall back on proven methods is understandable, even though those methods have been proven in a totally different context. In the short-term, construction output will continue to grow ahead of the local resource capacity. Therefore in the short run the 'best' solution will continue to incorporate the use of expatriate resources. The challenge is to increase local participation in line with a coherent strategy for developing the local construction capacity.

In allocating priority the conflict between public and private sector demand will have to be examined. This will involve a high level of intervention in a sector which does not easily lend itself to centalized control. The intention, however, is not to impose rigid limits on construction activity but rather to effect a marginal shift of resources between construction projects, and between construction and the rest of the economy.

REFERENCES TO APPENDIX

1 Based on B. Balkenhol, 'Small contractors: Untapped potential or economic impediment?', mimeographed *World Employment Programme Research Working Paper*, restricted (Geneva, ILO, 1979).
2 Based on J. Capt and G. A. Edmonds, 'Study of small contractors in Kenya', mimeographed *World Employment Programme Research Working Paper*, restricted (Geneva, ILO, 1977).
3 G. A. Edmonds, 'Small firms in the construction industry', MSc thesis, United Kingdom, University of Leeds, 1972.
4 Based on S. Drewer, 'Institutional constraints to the choice of appropriate construction technology', mimeographed *World Employment Programme Research Working Paper*, restricted (Geneva, ILO, 1982).

www.ingramcontent.com/pod-product-compliance
Ingram Content Group UK Ltd.
Pitfield, Milton Keynes, MK11 3LW, UK
UKHW021831140426
5217IPUK00021B/1385